STORIES
From
PROPHET'S LIFE

DR. ABDUR RAUF

ILLUSTRATED
BIOGRAPHY OF THE HOLY PROPHET
FOR CHILDREN AND BEGINNERS

FEROZSONS (Pvt.) LTD.
LAHORE-RAWALPINDI-KARACHI

Published by Ferozsons (Pvt.) Ltd.,
60, Shahrah-e-Quaid-e-Azam, Lahore, Pakistan
277, Peshawar Road, Rawalpindi
Mehran Heights, Main Clifton Road, Karachi

Ferozsons (Pvt.) Ltd. Registered Office:
60, Shahrah-e-Quaid-e-Azam, Lahore, Pakistan

First published in Pakistan 1990

Typeset in 13 on 15 point Times by
Ferozsons (Pvt.) Ltd., Lahore

Printed and bound in Pakistan by
Ferozsons (Pvt.) Ltd., Lahore

ISBN   969 0 10050 5

To
him (peace be upon him),
the greatest benefactor of humanity

CONTENTS

sonal Life *How the Magic Was Nullified? *Recitation of Anti-Magic Panacea *The Prophet Feels Unshackled *Magic and Its Impact on Prophets *A Factual, Historical Episode

16

DEATH OF THE GREAT BELOVED

153

*Agonies of Death Disease *"Abu Bakr Not Umar" *His Last Day on Earth *Last Words and Last Kisses *Confusion Before Burial *Last Wash and Last Glimpses *Moving Burial Episodes

LIST OF PICTURES AND MAPS

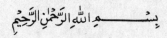

INTRODUCTION

The inspiring biography of Prophet Muhammad (pbuh) is profusely punctuated by fascinating events and episodes. STORIES FROM PROPHET'S LIFE is a carefully-selected presentation of the main events happening in Prophet's life span in such a manner that readers of all ages may enjoy stimulating accounts of the major roles played by the most charismatic character in human history.

Some of these stories were published in the newspapers and magazines. Ever since their appearance in the print media there have been persistent demands for their publication in the form of a book. In addition to its present English edition the book is also being presented in Urdu. Incidentally the book is an award-winner.

The basic object of the book is to portray the entire life of the Holy Prophet, from birth to death, in the form of interesting stories. The idea is to enable the readers to develop a correct and compact picture of the Seerat in a pleasant, yet thought-provoking, manner. From this novel angle this story book enjoys a distinctive and pioneering place in the entire gamut of the Seerat literature.

1

STORY OF A WONDERFUL BABY

Spring is a wonderful time. New saplings sprout up in the gardens. Fragrant flowers bloom forth all over. Colourful birds twitter about on the twigs, chirping ever sweet songs. Waves of smiles and happiness dominate everywhere. Dry and desolate lands begin to wear a gay and green look. The blissful spirit of health and happiness cheers even the most dull and the depressed faces.

As the days pass by spring's radiance begins to fade and wane. Flowers wither away. Gardens soon look deserted. Then a day comes when flowers cease to emit fragrance and no birds sing on the trees. Until the next spring people are obliged to wait for the radiance of hope and happiness.

An Ever-Fragrant Flower

Over fourteen hundred years ago a wonderful spring had come to the people of the world. That spring had never withered away. During that unforgettable spring a sweet little flower had bloomed whose fragrance was simply reanimating. Spring comes and goes away. Then hot summer sets in. Autumn gives a depressing look. Cold waves surge right and left during winter. Life then seems to be deserting all plants and trees. Birds cease to chirp. Depression and dullness grip the minds of men.

But that memorable spring was quite different. No change was visible in the ever-increasing freshness of that wonderous spring and its radiant flower. Its fragrance kept on multiplying day by day. Waves of mild wind then carried the seeds and saplings of that fascinating flower to all gardens of the globe. Soon every part of the world was blossoming with a marvellous species of flowers whose freshness and fragrance were immortal. Around such stimulating flowers sweet birds never ceased to sing songs of life and love. Their mallowing melodies bestowed vigour and vitality upon everyone around. Then a day dawned when that wonderful spring and its ever-fragrant flower transformed the very shape and temper of all humanity.

That unique flower still adores the gardens of the universe. People from all parts of the world relish its freshness. Years have rolled by since that spring flower bloomed. Its radiant fragrance has never ceased to increase and inspire.

Humanity is now unanimous to acknowledge that such a marvellous flower has neither bloomed before nor shall one like it ever bloom anywhere on this planet. The story of that wonderous flower is novel as well as stimulating.

2

Birth of a Blissful Being

That lovely flower bloomed forth in Makkah, the famed town of the Arabian peninsula, during a memorable spring. According to the local calendar it was Monday, 12th Rabi al-Awwal, the Year of the Elephant. The date, according to the Christian calendar, was April 22, 571 A.D. That was the august birthday of Prophet Muhammad (pbuh), the best of the humans ever born anywhere on earth.

His father was Abdullah and mother, Amina. Abdullah was an exceptionally good-natured man. Like her illustrious husband Amina too was a lady of high virtues. Prophet's grandfather, Abdul Muttalib, was leader of the famed Quraish tribe and the honoured chief of Makkah. Prophet Muhammad thus had an exceptionally-noble ancestry on paternal as well maternal sides.

It was customary in Arabia during those days that after the marriage the bridegroom stayed for sometime at bride's residence. Accordingly, Abdullah stayed at Amina's home for three days after their marriage. Then he returned to his own home along with his noble wife. After sometime he set out for Syria on a trade trip. On return he stayed at Madina. He fell sick there and died after a short while. He was buried at Madina.

When the sad news of his demise reached Makkah grief gripped Amina's household. She went into a spell of acute depression and dejection. Chief Abdul Muttalib too was shocked by the untimely demise of his virtuous son.

3

Feasts and Jubilations

Time rolled on. After sometime a bright male baby was born to lady Amina. This lessened considerably her load of grief and depression.

When Prophet's grandfather heard the news of the birth his joy knew no bounds. Winding up all engagements of the day he dashed to the residence of his noble daughter-in-law. He picked up the blessed baby in his arms and gave him a warm hug. Kissing him all the way he went straight to Kaabah. He expressed his gratitude to God and prayed for health and happiness of the new-born babe. Then he returned to Amina's house and replaced the baby in her lap gently. After considerable thinking he named the baby as Muhammad. This is a sweet Arabic word meaning, "the praised one". Although such unusual names were not in vogue at that time yet the great old chief felt pleased to choose it for his bright-looking grandson.

On the seventh day after the birth chief Abdul Muttalib sacrificed a nice camel and threw a big feast for the Quraish gentry. After the feast some curious guests inquired about the preference of a rather unusual name over the customary pattern of naming common in the area. To this Abdul Muttalib replied: "I wish the baby to be worthy of praise and appreciation of God and His people in heavens and on earth".

Search for a Foster Mother

According to the customs prevalent among the Makkan elites a few days after birth the new-born babies were entrusted to the custody of rural womenfolk who specialized in the art of nursing the babies. Such desert-living ladies would visit Makkah periodi-

The historic house in Makkah (left) where Prophet Muhammad
(pbuh) was born.

cally in caravans to carry away foster babies of their choices. They would then engage themselves in their feeding and upbringing in the free and bracing environment of the desert. When the foster babies grew a bit older they were returned to their parents. Foster mothers were rewarded by parents for their services.

A few days after Prophet's birth a caravan of foster mothers hailing from the neighbouring desert had entered Makkah city in search of foster babies. Old and emaciated Haleema Saadia was one of those in that group of foster mothers. It so happened that virtually everyone succeeded in getting a baby. Haleema, however, was still without one. In fact, lady Amina had discussed the proposition of her baby's adoption with practically every foster mother. Everyone, however, had declined to adopt baby Muhammad. They had apprehended that the prospects of reward in the deal of an orphan foster child were rather bleak and dubious.

When Amina tried to persuade Haleema for the job she too felt quite reluctant. After all what shall she do with a fatherless child in the lap of a helpless widow? How would a widow manage to pay proper remuneration for the painstaking services of a foster mother? As those calculations and apprehensions weighed rather heavily with Haleema she too had refused to adopt baby Muhammad despite the fact that she happened to be the only foster mother who had failed to get hold of any baby.

All the deals for foster babies over the caravan soon began to prepare for a retreat to the desert. Haleema's lap was as empty as ever before. She was in a fix. She held hurried consultations with Harith, her equally good-natured husband. Why not adopt Muhammad whom none was willing to carry? Something was certainly better than nothing. Instead of returning home empty-handed why not take a poor child? Harith appreciated the idea. Supporting his wife's proposal he said, "yes, I agree with you. Who knows this measure may be a blessing in disguise for us." Accordingly Haleema went back to lady Amina. The matter was settled amicably and Haleema picked up baby Muhammad.

Lean Pony and Old Camel

After the formal agreement Haleema and Harith began to pack up for the return journey along with the rest of the caravan. They had only a lean pony for riding and an old she-camel for milk. At that time Makkah's neighbourhood was in tight grips of severe drought and famine. Animal fodder was hard to find. While on way to Makkah Haleema had experienced great hardship in riding her lean and famished pony. Throughout the journey she had lagged behind her fellow-travellers again and again. She had been the butt of their jokes and taunts for the annoyingly-sluggish pace her famished pony had kept all along the way.

The deal having been struck with lady Amina, Haleema had picked up Muhammad. When she hugged the bright baby she was amazed to find that her erstwhile dry breast became wet all of a sudden. Baby Muhammad sucked her breast to his full. Along with him Haleema's own son and now Muhammad's foster brother, also had the mother's milk to his satisfaction. Their tummies full with milk the two babies slept peacefully. Haleema felt amazed as well as happy over

7

the unexpected shape of things. She remembered full well that the previous night she had to keep awake because her hungry baby, who could not be breast-fed, had been crying all the time. He could not be fed on old she-camel's milk either as she too was dry.

As Harith went near the aging she-camel he found her udders overflowing with milk. When milked it gave plenty of the stuff. Both he and his wife drank to their entire satisfaction. That night they enjoyed quite a peaceful sleep.

Waking up next morning the first thing Harith said was: "Haleema, I have begun to realize that the baby in our custody appears to be some blessed soul because we are being showered with Divine bounties ever since we adopted him". When they were all set for the return journey Haleema rode her lean pony and took baby Muhammad in her lap. They then joined the retreating caravan of the foster mothers.

It so happened that the very lean pony which while coming to Makkah had been lagging behind began to trot faster and faster. It ran ahead of all others. So much so that the other women had to shout again and again: "O Haleema, be steady. That does not seem to be the same lean and lanky pony on whom you started your journey with us when we had set out for Makkah." Haleema's repeated assurances that it was the same animal would convince none.

Towards the sunset that memorable day Haleema reached her tent in the desert safe and sound with baby Muhammad clinging firmly to her breast.

QUESTIONS

1.   Where and when was Prophet Muhammad born?

2. Who were his father and mother?
3. How did Muhammad's father die?
4. Describe the festivities and jubilations on Muhammad's birth?
5. Why did chief Abdul Muttalib name his grandson as "Muhammad"?
6. What for did foster mothers from the desert come to Makkah city?
7. What happened to Haleema's lean pony and she-camel after she had adopted baby Muhammad?

2

LITTLE MUHAMMAD'S EARLY CHILDHOOD

Carrying baby Muhammad in her lap Haleema Saadia eventually arrived at her ancestral village in the desert. The surrounding area being hit by a severe drought that year the shepherds experienced great difficulties in finding fodder for their herds. Consequently they were facing an acute milk shortage. Strange enough when Haleema's goats returned home from the neighbouring pastures they overflowed with milk. When others milked their goats they seldom got any worthwhile yield. Haleema's household had no such milk problem. Both the spouses as well as the children had plenty of the milk to drink.

All other shepherds of the desert village began to feel envious of Haleema's wonderful goats. They would send their goats to the very pastures where Haleema's goats grazed. But that wouldn't make any difference. Their goats returned as unfed and as hungry as ever before. None would yield beyond a few drops of milk. Soon the rumour began to gain currency that there was something mysteriously-blissful in the bright baby that Haleema had adopted.

Five Years in Desert

Haleema had a good-natured daughter, Sheema by name. She had developed a great liking for baby Muhammad. It was she who looked after him most of the time. Twice every year Haleema would take the baby to Makkah. After showing him to her mother and near relatives she would return to her desert tent. At the age of two he was weaned off. He looked quite a bright, handsome baby. Haleema took him to his mother.

By now Haleema had been thoroughly convinced that the orphan baby whom none was willing to adopt was in fact a wonderful creature. She had developed intense affection for the sweet little fellow. In fact she intended to keep him with her for some more time. Accordingly, she expressed her desire before Amina. Endorsing her request Haleema said, "baby Muhammad has reacted nicely to the free environment of the desert. Makkah is currently in the grips of an epidemic. It would, therefore, be far better if you permit the sweet baby to stay with me for some more time".

Her pleading was so forceful and grounds so convincing that lady Amina agreed readily to part company with her loving son for some more time to come. So baby Muhammad returned with Haleema to spend some more days in the free and open atmosphere of the desert. As he grew up he often used to go out shepherding with his foster brothers. Besides this early training in shepherding young Muhammad also enjoyed the same experience during later life. For

11

quite a few years he herded the goats of his tribe and of some other Makkans. While shepherding he got ample opportunities to ponder over the purpose of human life and the meaning of the universe. He used to make proud references to those wonderful days and thanked God for his enriching experiences.

Little Muhammad Lost in Makkah

When little Muhammad was five Haleema thought it advisable to return him to his mother. Taking the child along she arrived at Makkah. Unfortunately, however, the boy got lost in the conjestion of Makkan streets. Haleema was terribly upset. She searched the child in all directions but failed to find him anywhere. Shocked and exhausted she rushed to chief Abdul Muttalib. With tears trickling down her eyes she reported the matter to him.

Abdul Muttalib was taken aback. Praying for a speedy recovery of the lost child he dashed to the Holy Kaabah. Hardly had he reached there when Varqa b. Naufal and another youth of the Quraish met him. They were carrying little Muhammad. They reported that they had found the child strolling about in the Makkan hills. Abdul Muttalib thanked them. Then he perched the child on his shoulder and started going round the Kaabah, praying all the time for health and safety of his grandson. After a while he sent the child to his mother.

Mother's Death During Travel

Lady Amina was mighty pleased to greet his young son. Little Muhammad started living happily with his mother at their Makkan residence. A good-natured lady. Umme Aiman, was engaged as a nurse to look after him. When he was about six his mother thought of taking him to Madina in order to introduce him to his maternal uncles as also to visit his father's grave over there. So one fine morning the party composed of Muhammad, his mother, Amina, grandfather Abdul Muttalib and nurse Umme Aiman set out towards Madina.

They stayed at Madina for about a month. Little Muhammad was shown the house where his illustrious father had died while returning from Syria. The grief-stricken mother must have narrated him some events and episodes about his father's life. Consequently young Muhammad appeared to have grown considerably conscious of his orphanhood. After a brief stay the party set out for Makkah. Unfortunately, however, while still on the way Muhammad's loving mother fell ill and breathed her last at village Abwa. She was buried in the same village.

What a terrible shock for little Muhammad! He was drenched in tears on the sudden demise of his caring mother. He had often seen her shedding tears in seclusion over the depressing death of his father. Now when she too departed leaving him all alone in the midst of a long journey the bitter burden of orphanhood loomed heavier than ever before over his innocent mind. He presented a pathetic picture of agony and anguish. Incessant tears rolled down his cheeks in torrents. Nurse Umme Aiman endeavoured hard to dry the copious tears of the non-plussed child. Consoling him all the way she managed to tow him back to their home in Makkah.

The historic house of Prophet's birth now housing a Government office.

Unforgettable Childhood Memories

During that traumatic journey little Muhammad's stay at Madina was obviously very brief. However, many childhood experiences of those days left their indelible impression on his fertile mind. Many years later when once he passed by Madina past memories and old affections seemed to have resurrected all of a sudden. He pointed towards a house and said, "that's the house where my mother had stayed in". Seeing a pond he cried with joy, "I learnt swimming here in this pond". Raising his finger towards an open field he remarked gleefully, "this is the field where I used to play with little Aneesa".

Similarly loving memories of Haleema and Umme Aiman never faded in freshness. In later life whenever Haleema visited him he used to stand up in reverence. He would often embrace her shouting out gleefully: "my mother, my mother!" He would spread his mantle for her and would remain standing until she sat down. Indeed he would address her with such an over doze of honour and affection that the spectators felt amazed and envious.

Once drought caused famine in Makkah. Haleema visited the Prophet those days. He extended her all respects and courtesies. When she was about to leave he presented her a gift of a fine camel and four goats. At another occasion Haleema's daughter, Sheema was brought before him as a prisoner of war along with some others. He extended her extraordinary affection and courtesies. In compliance with Sheema's wish he arranged her speedy repatriation to her tribe.

QUESTIONS

1. What blissful changes did Haleema enjoy in her household after her adoption of baby Muhammad?
2. Why did she want to keep the baby with her for some more time?
3. What was the impact of early shepherding experiences on Prophet's life?
4. How was baby Muhammad lost and found in the Makkah city?
5. How did Muhammad's mother die?
6. What did nurse Umme Aiman do on the death of Prophet's mother?
7. How did the Prophet cherish the fond memories of his brief stay at Madina as a child along with his loving mother?
8. What affections and courtesies did he shower over his foster mother and her family?

3

STORY OF A LOVELY SHEPHERD

On the untimely demise of young Muhammad's mother the honour of looking after him fell rather exclusively to the lot of his grandfather, Abdul Muttalib. He undertook that responsibility with great affection and dedication. Unfortunately, however, poor Muhammad had not yet recovered from the trauma of his loving mother's death when his noble grandfather also breathed his least. The young boy was hardly eight then. His infancy was punctuated by a rapid succession of tearful tragedies. When he joined his grandfather's funeral procession torrential tears trickled down his innocent cheeks. The lovely little boy presented a pathetic picture of grief and depression.

After the death of the great old man one of his sons and little Muhammad's uncle, Abu Talib, undertook to look after his orphan nephew. Accordingly he began to discharge his obligations with utmost affection and fortitude. He showered far more affection and love over the young boy than even his own children.

Shepherding and Human Guidance

The first regular vocation that young Muhammad chanced to learn was herdsmanship. He had made initial ventures into this noble field even while residing in the desert home of his foster mother. Subsequently, he got further experience of herding the goats of his family and some other Makkans as well.

In later life he always referred to this exciting and instructive early experience as one of the Divine bounties. He used to say: "Herdsmanship is an essential pre-requisite for Prophethood. The office of the Prophet is unattainable without prior experience of herdsmanship. I have also herded the goats of my family".

The life of a shepherd is full of fascinating experiences. It is simply exciting and enchanting. Driving his herd as he sets forth towards open environments he gets vast and varied opportunities of observing nature and reflecting on life during various shepherding exercises. Sprawling greenery, lofty trees and mysterious shrubs with a canopy of the blue sky overhead present an ideal physical setting not available in any other profession. The refreshing setting stimulates creative thinking and constructive behaviour. The process of tending the cattle, managing their food and planning their security and safe return calls for high level of originality and insight.

Such meaningful shepherding schedules generate vital developmental incentives. They provide the much-needed food for the body and soul of a perceiving shepherd. In more exceptional and more creative cases such dynamic incentives get widened in their scope. The shepherd feels intrigued to extend the sphere of his experiences and exercises to cover larger and larger segments of the needy humanity. The original process of pasturing the cattle then assumes newer and vaster dimensions. If thoughtfully engineered such trends transform themselves into tending and guiding people to a really-purposeful destiny. Wholesome panaceas to safeguard the baffled mankind against all ills and evils begin to flow from the fertile imagination of such a conscientious shepherd. That is how a great shepherd's professional experiences eventually prepare him for the wonderous office of human guidance under the Divine scheme of things.

When that vital stage arrives and the resultant transformation of human life takes shape the shepherd stands out as a real blessing and a real saviour of all civilization and culture.

The Shepherd and the Story-Tellers

Prophet Muhammad's life is full of an unending chain of creative ideas and constructive deeds. Makkah's merry-making life style had failed to influence his blessed body and sacred soul. At that time story-telling was a common pastime in the Arabian peninsula. Large groups of professional story-tellers had sprung up in Makkah as well. After day's labour mirthful crowds would assemble at popular public places. Seasoned story-tellers would then start chains of fascinating tales and annecdotes. Such an all-engaging activity often continued throughout the night. Keen listeners enjoyed those spicy folk tales in rapt attention and with unfading gusto.

Once during early years young Muhammad had also cherished strong desires to attend one such nightly story-telling session. As he went in search of the same he got distracted on the way by the hullabaloo of a noisy marriage function. Accordingly, he stopped to enjoy that colourful event. But the moment he entered the wedding house a curious state of prolonged sleep spell overtook him rather all of a sudden.

Shepherd Muhammad Seeking Recreation

Prophet Muhammad's memoirs pertaining to the period of shepherding are interesting as well as instructive. One such episode has been narrated by the Prophet himself in these words: "I had no inherent attraction for all those pleasant pastimes that the Makkan pagans indulged in so fondly. On two occasions even when I had intended to enjoy those recreations God intervened in between me and my desires. Once I and another shepherd from the Quraish were tending our cattle over the hills of Makkah. I told my colleague that I was going to the city for the night in quest for some rest and recreation.....I requested him to take care of my goats as well. When the other shepherd consented I set out for the city. As I neared the very first house sweet melodies of flute and tambourine struck my ears. I was told that the inmates were busy celebrating a wedding function. I too went in and sat among them. I had hardly started enjoying the music when God suddenly shut my ears. Sound slumbers of sweet sleep overwhelmed me so completely that only the rays of the following morning's sun could wake me up. I remained utterly unaware of the proceedings of that merry marriage party. Then I hastened to return to my companion in the hilly pasture and reported him the entire episode".

Narrating the other event the Prophet reports: "Similarly, once again precisely the same thing happened when I set out for the Makkah city for a similar purpose. Some musical notes had struck my ears all of a sudden. I felt as if it was a heavenly melody. But that very moment deep sleep overtook me suddenly. I remained asleep till the next morning. After that I never conceived of such ideas till Prophethood was conferred on me".

Interesting Memoirs of a Great Shepherd

It is hard to visualize the heights of the character and personality of a healthy man who abstains from all sorts of distractions and deviations during his fiery youth. Wherein, afterall, lies the harm in enjoying interesting stories and sweet music for a little while after a full days hard toil as a busy shepherd? In the Divine scheme of things, however, even such an otherwise permissible leisure appeared to be ruled out in the case of that lovely shepherd. Fun and frolic could hardly find any worthwhile place in the life schedule of a blissful being about to be entrusted with the all-too exalted office of guidance and salvation of the entire human stock. As patent on the annals of human history the entire shepherding period of Prophet Muhammad was spent exclusively in creative meditation and constructive deeds.

Later on during the Prophethood period he used to refer to simple and serene vocation of herdsmanship with considerable pride and pleasure. Once he chanced to pass through a forest with some of his companions. The companions began to eat small plums growing on a tree. The Prophet remarked: "Only those plums which turn dark enough are sweeter. I discovered this while shepherding during childhood when I used to graze my goats right here".

QUESTIONS

1. How did the Prophet feel on the death of his grandfather?
2. How did his uncle, Abu Talib, look after him after his grandfather's death?
3. Describe the Prophet's early experiences of shepherding.
4. How did Prophet's wish to enjoy the nightly story-telling sessions remain unfulfilled?
5. How did the Prophet relish memories of his early experiences as a shepherd?

4

THE SWEET SHEPHERD TURNS TRADER

Like the affectionate grandfather uncle Abu Talib also was unusually fond of young Muhammad. The orphan boy was dearer to him than even his own children. The cordial uncle-nephew ties had grown so strong that for quite a long period of time little Muhammad preferred to sleep with his loving uncle. He would always accompany him wherever he went. Seldom were the two seen separate.

First Travel to Syria

The clan of Quraish were basically traders by vocation. They always remained immersed in some sort of a trade and commerce in and outside their homeland. When Muhammad was twelve Abu Talib began to pack up for a trade trip to Syria. As travel was extremely hazardous those days he was reluctant to take Muhammad along with him. The sweet nephew, however, insisted too much and clung fast to him till the loving uncle gave in. Accompanying his uncle young

A traditional Arab caravan on way to Syria.

Muhammad joined the trade caravan. Together they proceeded as far as Basra, a town on the north of Syria.

At Basra the caravan halted near a church. Bahirah was the wise monk of that church. When he saw young Muhammad he told Abu Talib that his illustrious nephew possessed all those signs and salients of Prophethood which had been mentioned in sacred books of the Christians. Monk Bahirah apprehended that the Syrian Jews would identify immediately those clear-cut signs of Prophethood so manifest on Muhammad's bright forehead. The vicious Jews might then conspire to harm the young boy. Accordingly he advised the caravan leaders not to let Muhammad proceed further. Realizing the delicacy of the situation Abu Talib accepted Bahirah's advice. He, therefore, sold his entire merchandize rather hurriedly and dashed back to Makkah along with Muhammad.

During that memorable trip young Muhammad got ample opportunities to study nature and people. He reflected over various aspects of the human psyche. Although he was raw in years he held quite worthwhile discussions with leaders of different religions. They were all impressed by the deep insight of a young boy of that tender age.

Abu Talib could not make any profit out of that trade trip. Consequently, he never even thought of foreign trade again after that discouraging experience. He had some capital with him. He managed to spend his remaining life within the four walls of Makkah. During that period young Muhammad continued to live with him. He used to graze his goats and helped him in the domestic chores. He spent most of his leisure hours listening to the verses of the famed Arab poets as recited in the streets of Makkah. He would weigh and evaluate addresses of various religious speakers whom he chanced to listen. For considerable spells of time he also remained engrossed in secluded meditation.

Muhammad Trades for Khadijah

Abu Talib's household was vexed with monetary worries. Sweet Muhammad was by now a fine young man of twenty-five. Although their earlier Syrian trade venture had flopped, in the heart of his hearts Abu Talib still wished his loving nephew to switch over from herdsmanship to trading on a permanent basis. He was on the look out for an appropriate opportunity for the desired vocational shift.

During those days there lived in Makkah a prosperous and a famed widow, Khadijah. She happened to be Muhammad's cousin by relation. Because of the purity of her character people referred to her by the title of Tahira, which means 'the pious lady'. She was a seasoned trader. She used to engage honest and intelligent tradesmen on remunerative basis for her commercial trips and transactions. She had heard much of young Muhammad's widespread reputation for piety, honesty and wisdom. Khadijah presented Muhammad a proposal to sell her merchandize in Syria on commission basis. Young Muhammad accepted the offer. When everything was settled Muhammad set out for a second time on his trade mission to Syria. Khadijah also sent her slave, Maysara, to accompany Muhammad on the trip.

In addition to his earlier knowledge of Syria

young Muhammad had acquired considerably vast trade experience in several other famed commercial centres. Yamen was one of the countries where lady Khadijah had also deputed him on trade missions. He went there twice. Each time Khadijah gave him one camel as his remuneration. But of all the trade journeys undertaken by him the second trade trip to Syria enjoys considerable significance in his personal history.

During that famous trip he earned unusually big profits. But along with his successful commercial transaction he also kept on thinking on the real meaning and purpose of human life. He engaged in fruitful discussions with leaders of various religions. During that trade trip Khadijah's personal slave, Maysara, too had the opportunity of watching him rather closely. He was greatly impressed by his commercial integrity and insight on the one hand and the exceptional calibre of his general behaviour on the other.

Seeds of Attraction and Love

On return home young Muhammad presented lady Khadijah a report of the journey. He apprised her of all the commercial transactions and handed over all the resultant profits. The unusual fairness of the young trader impressed Khadijah very much. Later on Maysara also apprised her of his impressions about the charismatic character and personality of young Muhammad. In fact, he told her plainly that there was hardly any other young man in Makkah who could excel Muhammad in moral fibre and intellectual calibre. Seeds of love and attraction for fascinating Muhammad had by then been sown rather far too deeply in the mind of lady Khadijah.

Straight dealing and wise handling of business affairs had yielded considerable satisfaction to young Muhammad. The transition from herdsmanship to tradesmanship expanded further the universe of his worldly experience and insight. This sharpened further the prospects of his impending role as a great guide destined to teach humanity the art of a magic trade. That "trade" never failed to fetch inestimable profits in all sectors of life.

QUESTIONS

1. Why did monk Bahirah advise the caravan leaders not to take Muhammad further on the trade trip?
2. Why couldn't Abu Talib make any profits out of the Syrian trade trip?
3. Why did he want his nephew to switch over from herdsmanship to tradesmanship?
4. Why did Lady Khadijah select Muhammad to trade for her?
5. What did Muhammad do on return from the second Syrian trade trip?
6. Why was Khadijah impressed by young Muhammad so much?

5

MUHAMMAD MARRIES KHADIJAH

L ady Khadijah was already all praise for young Muhammad's moral calibre and charismatic personality. The experience of pleasant commercial dealings strengthened further her preliminary impressions. Seeds were sowed in her mind for respect, affection and attraction for the impressive and inspiring young man.

The Pious Lady

Khadijah was the daughter of Khuwalid b. Asad. She was first married to Abu Hala, who died after two sons had been born to the couple. She was then married to a wealthy Makkan trader, Atiq b. Aaid Makhzoomi. After the birth of a daughter the second husband too expired. Khadijah was a graceful widow of forty when she came in contact with Muhammad.

She was an exceptionally-charming person. Her sound moral reputation had earned her the honoured title of 'Tahira', 'the pious lady'. Lately, quite a large number of eminent chiefs of the Quraish had desired to marry her. But she had turned down their proposals. Young Muhammad's moral integrity impressed her most. Like her he too had earned the honoured title of 'Ameen', which means, 'the trustworthy'. So a pious lady decided to marry a trustworthy young man.

According to the traditions of the times the Arab womenfolk enjoyed the privilege of initiating and negotiating their own matrimonial affairs. Khadijah took the initiative boldly. Taking her close friend, Nafeesa, into confidence she told her everything.

The Marriage Solemnized

Nafeesa was a wise woman. She held an immediate meeting with Muhammad. "Why don't you get married?" Nafeesa put him the straight question. The Prophet replied, "I don't have the requisite resources". Nafeesa said, "if a beautiful, graceful and resourceful lady, hailing from an honoured family desires to marry you, would you accept the proposal?" The Prophet asked Nafeesa to disclose the name of the person under reference. On learning that it was Khadijah he consented readily.

Other formalities were covered soon and a date fixed for the marriage. The Prophet arrived at Khadijah's residence along with his kinsfolk. The wedding ceremonies went into operation. Abu Talib delivered the wedding sermon. The bride's dowery was fixed at twenty young she-camels. According to the prevalent custom after the marriage the Prophet stayed at Khadijah's residence. With the advent of married life his involvement in meditation increased considerably. His participation in reform and guidance of people also began to register an upward trend.

Hadrat Khadijah's ancestral home (left) at Makkah.

An Ideal Marriage

Lady Khadijah was full fifteen years senior to Prophet Muhammad. But because both the spouses had attained to a unique level of mental and moral maturity the difference of age did not stand in the way of mutual adjustment and marital love. The marriage rather proved an ideal one. Their home earned an unusual reputation for health and happiness.

Lady Khadijah lived for twenty-five years after their blissful marriage. Each moment of the marital life was replete with mutual affection and regards. They were blessed with six children. Of these two sons died during early infancy. The names of the four surviving daughters are: Fatimah, Zainab, Ruqayyah and Umme Kulthoom. The Prophet loved his wife and all their children immensely.

Even after Khadijah's death he never ceased to remember her with extreme affection and respect. Long after her death once while paying her tributes he is reported to have remarked: "She was an ideal wife. She accepted Islam when the whole of Arabia was pagan. She sacrificed her entire wealth for me." The Prophet even extended due courtesies and regards to Khadijah's folks and friends whenever they happened to meet him.

QUESTIONS

1. How was Lady Khadijah attracted towards the Prophet?
2. Why was she referred to by the title "Tahira"?
3. Why did people call the Prophet "Ameen"?
4. Describe the ceremonies of Prophet's marriage?
5. Why is it considered as an ideal marriage?
6. Name Prophet's children from Lady Khadijah?
7. How did the Prophet show affection and respect for his wife?

6

THE BLACK STONE
HULLABALOO

The Holy Kaabah is the centre of respect and veneration for all Muslims. It was first constructed by Prophet Adam (pbuh), the first citizen of the world. Angel Gabriel had brought a big black stone (Hajar al-Aswad) from the Paradise which was fixed in the structure. It is presently fixed in the south-eastern wall of the Kaabah. During Prophet Nooh's (pbuh) days the big typhoon washed it away. Only a small mound was left standing at the site. Prophet Ibraheem (pbuh) and his illustrious son, Prophet Ismaeel (pbuh) then rebuilt Kaabah under Divine instructions.

The Kaabah is variously named as Bait Ullah (House of God), Bait ul-Haram (Sacred House), Masjid al-Haram (Sacred Mosque), etc. All these names denote that it is a sacred place, meant only for the worship of One God. It has continued to enjoy great respect and reverence from times immemorial. People have been performing Hajj at Kaabah. Even cultural congregations and colourful festivals have been held

A view of the life pattern around Holy Kaabah during ancient Arabia.

around it. With the passage of time, however, Kaabah got deteriorated into a temple for idol worship. During Prophet Muhammad's early period it was housing a panoramic variety of 360 idols. Each Arab tribe had its own idol to worship. But even then there were quite a few insightful people who declined to bow before man-made idols. Prophet Muhammad was one such wise person.

Damage by Rains and Floods

The Kaabah is situated in a low-lying area of Makkah. During olden times rain and flood water used to stagnate around it. This caused considerable damage to its boundary walls and even inner structures. In order to prevent accumulation of water a small dam-like structure had been constructed outside the Kaabah. But that too did not work. Breaking again and again by raging waters the frail dam had eventually got demolished with the passage of time. Thereafter the damage rate to the building went on increasing. The process of continuous damage reached a precarious stage when it began to appear as if the entire structure would collapse any moment.

The people of Makkah felt extremely concerned about the precarious situation. They planned to demolish the badly-dilapidated portions and to rebuild the super structure. But since times immemorial a strong belief had gained widespread currency that God's wrath would befall if any portion of the Holy Kaabah was demolished. Consequently, nobody had dared to undertake the much-needed repairs. Nevertheless, continuous floods and flow of the waste city water had damaged the boundary walls to such an

35

alarming extent that instant repairs appeared inevitable to avert the impending collapse. The Makkans were in a real fix.

Prophet Muhammad was thirty-five then. He had earned a great reputation for his sociable disposition. In constructive social welfare projects he always collaborated with his Makkan compatriots. He too was naturally worried about the urgency of repairing the Kaabah in time. He rather felt the urgency more sensitively than anyone else.

Theft of Kaabah's Treasures

The urgency of the requisite repairs to Kaabah was heightened by many other related factors as well. There used to be a big pit in the middle of the Kaabah. Visitors used to throw their offerings in that pit. Lately, someone had stolen considerable quantity of precious objects from it. The thief had an easy go because the Kaabah walls were low and fragile. There was no roof overhead either.

The stolen articles were eventually recovered from Duwayk, a freed man of Makkah. The enraged Quraish cut off his hands in punishment. Repairing the walls and even laying a proper roof overhead now appeared all the more inevitable to prevent further plundering of the treasures in the pit.

The Python and the Eagle

Another interesting episode was also responsible for priority attention to the matter. Around that pit lived a big python. During daylight it would crawl out and sit on Kaabah's wall to enjoy fresh air and sunshine. If anyone neared it, it spread its hood, started

Then suddenly an eagle swooped over the cobra and flew away with it.

hissing in a frightening posture and lept furiously to bite. Accordingly nobody dared to face the terror.

The nerve-shattering fear of that dreadful python also stood in the way of Kaabah's repairs and reconstruction. Luckily one day an eagle chanced to fly over that area. It pounced upon the basking python and flew away with it. After the end of the python the Makkans began to feel as if God had cleared the way for the reconstruction of the Holy Kaabah.

The interesting event has been depicted in the following verses by poet Zubair:

"I was amazed that the eagle went straight
To the snake when it was excited.
It used to rustle ominously
And sometimes it would dart forth.
When we planned to rebuild the Kaabah
It terrified us for it was fearsome.
When we feared its attack, down came the eagle,
Deadly straight in its swoop,
It bore it away, thus leaving us free
To work without further hindrance.
We attacked the building together,
We had its foundations and the earth.
On the morrow we raised the foundation,
None of our workers wore clothes."

Greek Engineer's Supervision
It so happened that a Greek engineer, Baqum, was sailing those days on a trade trip around the Arabian peninsula. As his ship neared Jeddah it was caught up in a storm. It ran aground and got wrecked. Baqum was a talented engineer. He had considerable mastery over masonary and woodwork as well. When

The historic repairs in progress at the Holy Kaabah.

the Makkans came to know about the ship disaster they sent a deputation to Baqum. They bought the broken ship so that its wooden planks could be utilized in Kaabah's reconstruction. The deputation prevailed upon Baqum to come over to Makkah and to supervise the reconstruction work at the Kaabah. A trained local worker was also hired to assist Baqum and the great project got started with unusual enthusiasm.

All the tribes had united to engage in the historic project. Each tribe focused on its apportioned job enthusiastically. Prophet Muhammad also participated with his characteristic vigour and vitality.

Clouds of Strife and Bloodshed

The requisite building material was collected from all sources. Bluish stones were obtained from the hills surrounding Makkah. Everything began to be done quite meticulously and enthusiastically. When the walls had risen to their pevious height of about 5-6 feet the great step arrived to fix the Black Stone at its old place. Lifting the sacred stone and placing it at the proper point was such a great honour that every tribe yearned to pocket it unshared. This led to heated arguments and bitter altercations. No tribe was willing to forego its right to enjoy the unique honour. As the bitter dispute prolonged and tempers rose higher and higher the pugnacious tribes found themselves dragging to the verge of a bloody civil war. Swords were soon unsheathed and those savage folks appeared all set for a fierce feud.

One wary tribe went totally beyond limits. It declared that it would not at all allow any other tribe to share the honour. According to an old Arab custom

A recent view of the Holy Kaabah.

whenever someone had to vow in utter desperation to die for a serious cause he dipped his fingers in a special cup filled with human blood. The chief of that pugnacious tribe placed a cup full of blood right in the Kaabah. One by one all the fiery youths of that bloodthirsty tribe dipped their fingers into the cup, vowing firmly that if any other tribe dared to touch the Black Stone they would lay down their lives in a bid to annihilate the rival.

That horribly hot war of nerves had gripped all Makkans for full four days. It then appeared quite certain that an endless bloody civil war would erupt any moment.

The Saviour Saves the Situation

An aged leader of the Quraish displayed great wisdom and statesmanship. He wanted the Black Stone furore to settle amicably. He proposed that whosoever enters Kaabah from Safa Mount side the next morning be appointed as the arbitrator. Then whatever verdict he gave was to be accepted by all the wary tribes. Complete consensus prevailed over that wonderful proposal.

Next morning everyone sat outside the Kaabah and waited to see who entered first from the Safa side. Fortunately, the first man entering from that side was the Prophet himself. He had already earned the honoured titles of "Ameen" (trustworthy) and "Sadiq" (truthful). As people watched him stepping in they began to shout joyfully: "There comes 'the trusted one' whom we all know full well. We accept him as our arbitrator".

The Prophet was fully aware of the delicacy of the

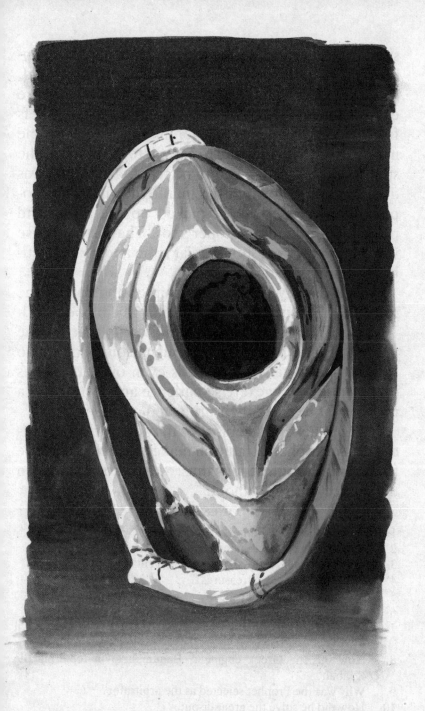

The Black Stone—a bloody feud over which was averted by Holy Prophet's statesmanship.

situation. He said, "bring me a mantle". It was supplied instantaneously. He spread it on the ground. Lifting the Black Stone he placed it gently in the centre of the mantle. Then he asked the representative chiefs from all the erstwhile belligerent tribes to hold the mantle from the sides and to carry it together up to the spot where the Stone had to be fixed. When that was done he said, "now put the mantle down". The Prophet then stepped forth, picked up the Stone and placed it firmly in its proper spot. The just and wise way he handled a controversial issue and a combustible situation satisfied everyone.

That display of statesmanship on the part of the great Prophet succeeded in warding off a bloody feud. Those belligerent tribesmen had literally reached the verge of a frightful civil war. A pugnacious people who were prone to take out swords even on petty issues could not possibly exercise patience and restraint in a matter that touched their pride and prestige.

The Black Stone episode enjoys historical significance. A Prophetic tradition makes a subtle reference to the great event. It runs thus: "I am the last stone in the edifice of Prophethood".

QUESTIONS

1. What is the Black Stone?
2. What are the various names of the Holy Kaabah?
3. Why did repairs to Kaabah appear urgent?
4. Who stole Kaabah's treasures?
5. How was the thief punished?
6. Narrate briefly the story of the python and the eagle?
7. What was driving the Arab tribes to the verge of a bloody civil war?
8. How did the Greek engineer, Baqum, help in repairing the Kaabah?
9. Why was the Prophet selected as the arbitrator?
10. How did he solve the great dispute?

7

MYSTERIOUS EVENTS AT THE HIRA CAVE

Three miles away from the city of Makkah rises the mountain Hira, now named as Jabal al-Noor (the Mountain of Light). On a side of this graceful mountain stands majestically one of the world's most famed caves, the Hira Cave. It is a small cave, 12 feet in length and about two feet in breadth. In his young days Prophet Muhammad used to visit the place rather too frequently. He used to stay there for hours and sometimes even for days together. There he engaged in meditation and prayers. He took enough quantity of ground barley and drinking water with him. When his stock of the simple ration was depleted he would return home and after some rest take more of the food stuff and went back to the cave to resume his meaningful schedule of prayers and meditation. With the passage of time his involvement in seclusion and introspection became more and more pronounced. He used to keep fasts as well. He reserved the entire month of Ramadan for fasts and spiritual purification. He took pleasure in feeding the hungry and helping the needy.

The Hira Cava, the venue of the first revelation.

Before returning home each time he made it a point to complete his round of the Kaabah.

During the spell of meditation at Cave Hira a wide panorama of pressing problems loomed large on his mind. He endeavoured hard to discover their adequate solutions. Occasionally he came out of the cave and after short strolls in the neighbouring forest returned to his favourite cave. He was seriously concerned about the idolatrous practices in vogue around him. From the very outset he had refused pointblank to appreciate or practise the prevalent style of pagan worship. As the time rolled on he started to have wonderous dreams which came true. Whatever he dreamt at night took place in the shape of factual reality the very next day.

Angel Meets the Prophet

The historic day was 9th Rabi ul-Awwal (12th February, 610 A.D.). He had completed his fortieth year. He was engaged as usual in his routine schedule of prayers and meditation inside the Hira Cave. Suddenly Angel Gibraeel entered in and said: "Muhammad, please accept felicitations. You are now a Messenger of God. I am Gibraeel."

This was the first ever communication sent to him from God. Consequently, the Prophet felt a bit apprehensive and nervous. Feeling uneasy he began to shiver. He returned home hurriedly. He lied down and asked his wife, Khadijah, to cover him with a mantle. After resting for a while he felt composed. He then narrated Khadijah the details of the strange incident at Hira. He further remarked: "I have been experiencing things which often frighten me. I fear lest I be posses-

47

sed by spirits".

Khadijah was seriously concerned about her loving husband. But she managed to hide her anxiety. She consoled him saying: "You have no cause to worry about. You are kind to your kinsfolk. You are truthful. You patronize widows, orphans and the needy. You are hospitable and sympathetic towards the afflicted people. God will never put a person of your standing to grief. No spirit whatsoever will obsess you".

Timely words of sympathy and comfort from an understanding wife consoled the Prophet considerably. But even a person of lady Khadijah's calibre had started feeling worried within. She felt that she too needed solace and comfort for her shaken self. Accordingly she took him to an understanding cousin, Várqa b. Naufal. He was an exceedingly virtuous, wise and well-versed figure of the day. Feeling disgusted with paganism prevailing in Makkah he had accepted Christianity. On Khadijah's insistence the Prophet narrated him all the facts of the Hira episode.

After listening attentively to Prophet's account Varqa said excitedly: "By God, you are in fact the Prophet of these people. There is no doubt about the fact that the great angel who came to you was the same one who had earlier visited Musa. Now on people will endeavour to falsify and torture you. You will be excommunicated. War will be waged against you. If I live to see that day I will side God's true faith". Then Varqa bowed his head in respect and kissed the middle of Prophet's head.

After a satisfying session with that insightful scholar Prophet Muhammad and Lady Khadijah returned

home. Varqa died a few days afterwards. The good old
fellow had grown too weak and had lost his vision.

Revelation Starts at Hira

After a lapse of about six months the Prophet was
engrossed one day in his usual round of prayers and
meditation inside the Hira Cave. The same angel visited him again. This time he held a piece of paper in his
hand. The angel said, "read." The Prophet enquired
in amazement, "what am I to read?." The angel embraced the Prophet and said again, "read." The
Prophet repeated, "what am I to read?" The angel
embraced him again saying , "read." The Prophet
gave him the same answer and the angel embraced him
the third time. The angel then helped the Prophet to
recite the following verses with him:

The Embryo
In the name of God, the Beneficent, the Merciful,
1. Read in the name of your Lord,
    Who created,
2. Created man from an embryo.

49

3. Read and your Lord is the Most Beneficent,
4. Who taught by the pen,
5. Taught man which he knew not.

(Surah: 96, Verses: 1−5)

The historic verses constitute the first Divine revelation to Prophet Muhammad. The blessings of knowledge for mankind and the necessity of its acquisition were thus stressed right from the very beginnings of the revelation. The recital over, the angel took the Prophet to the side of the mountain. There they performed ablution (wudu) and prayed together.

Propagation of Islam Begins

So the Prophet had by then received a clear-cut signal from God to go ahead with the noble mission of preaching Islam. Accordingly soon after returning home from the Hira Cave that day the Prophet started to disseminate the message of Islam. Those who accepted Islam the very first day included his wife Khadijah, cousin Ali, close friend Abu Bakr and personal slave Zaid b. Harith. These persons were too close to him. They knew him in and out. Their immediate acceptance of Islam also stands out as a glowing tribute to the nobility and purity of Prophet's charismatic character. As the process progressed further the Prophet utilized all decent and effective media of preaching and propagation. In order to introduce his kinsfolk to the beauties of Islam he often invited them to feasts at his home.

In the beginning Muslims were quite handful. Consequently they used to offer their prayers quietly and even secretly in the secluded sides of the Makkan mountains. After sometime the Prophet was instructed by God to preach Islam publicly. Gradually more and more people started to join the folds of Islam. One day the Prophet stood on Mount Safa and addressed his people publicly. In a dramatic and persuasive manner he extended them an open invitation to accept Islam.

When Swords Flashed on Him

Then a day came when the number of the pagans turning Muslims rose to about forty. The Prophet then went straight to the Kaabah and started preaching Islam. Highlighting the beauties of Islam he stressed the necessity and utility of believing in the Oneness of God. He admonished the audience to worship the One God rather than bowing before a multiplicity of man-made idols. This was his first public address in Kaabah in a characteristically bold manner.

The nasty pagans considered this as an open insult to their ancestral idols. They were all furious. A volcano of hatred and anger erupted all of a sudden. Everyone present in the Kaabah took out his sword. In a twinkling of the eye the Prophet was surrounded on all sides by hostile pagans.

A friend of the Prophet, Hadrat Harith Abu Hala, was inside his home that time. When the news of the great furore reached him he dashed forth to Kaabah. As he stepped forward in a bid to protect the Prophet a number of savage swords flashed on him. He was seriously injured. He fell and succumbed to his wounds. Abu Hala was thus the first martyr in Islam's path whose innocent blood was sprinkled over Kaabah's sacred soil.

QUESTIONS

1. What important role has Hira Cave played in the history of Islam?
2. What did the Prophet use to do there?
3. What did Angel Gibraeel tell the Prophet on his first meeting?
4. What did Varqa b. Naufal say when the Hira incident was related to him?
5. What was the first Divine revelation at Hira?
6. Who were those who were foremost in embracing Islam?
7. What did the Prophet tell the people while standing on Mount Safa?
8. What was Prophet's first sermon in the Kaabah?
9. What did the nasty pagans do after that sermon?
10. Who was the first martyr in the way of Islam?

8

PSYCHOLOGICAL OFFENSIVES
AGAINST THE PROPHET

As the Prophet's mission of spreading Islam be-came wider and its sphere of influence expanded the pagans of Makkah became more and more bitter in teasing and torturing him and his followers. Indeed those oppressive offensives were so numerous, so diversified and so painful that one shudders even to visualize them. When the pagans realized that sheer verbal opposition did not yield the desired results they endeavoured to trap him through the greed of power and wealth, peace and tranquillity. When these moves failed to work they conspired to excommunicate him and his followers. They threatened to wage bloody battles against him. Sieges were laid on the Muslims from all sides. They were boycotted economically and socially. The idea was to make them disgustful of their faith or weaken them through physical torture and extermination. Despite all opposition and harassment the Prophet and his followers clung fast to their cherished creed. They faced the unbearable situation with characteristic courage and fortitude. The more the enemy manoeuvres mounted high the more stead-fast did the Muslims grow in their patience and perse-verance, determination and dedication.

The enemy plans and projects of mental and phys-ical torture could be classified under three main categories:

(1) psychological offensives to defame and de-moralize,

(2) murderous conspiracies and deadly assaults, and

(3) playing black magic and dreadful witchcraft.

In the whole history of mankind Prophet Muham-mad's person stands out conspicuously as one whose life was a perpetual target of all sorts of violent at-tacks. Again, he is the only person who had narrow es-capes on all such deadly attempts at his life. Failing each time his enemies felt extreme frustration and frenzy. But they kept on chasing the man they wanted to kill by hook or by crook.

The details of their torturous plots are both in-teresting as well as instructive. Some of these were re-ally nerve-shattering. It was simply due to the insight, determination and endurance of the Prophet that these wild measures failed to achieve their intended targets. Rather than surrendering to the oppressive at-mosphere the Muslims stood like a firm rock. Conse-quently the evil forces were defeated on all fronts. Islam eventually emerged as a victorious system.

Being full of horror and harassment all of the above-referred categories of tortures and tribulations require a perspective appraisal. The present lines focus exclusively on the psychological war of nerves waged against the Prophet. The horrendous details of the murderous assaults will be dealt with separately. So will be the accounts of the Pagan-Jewish endeavours to kill the Prophet through black magic and witchery.

Some of the more conspicuous varieties of the psychological pranks and pressures and slanderous events and episodes are briefly described in the lines that follow.

Defaming the Prophet

The character and personality of the Holy Prophet were so charming that he had earned the most honoured titles of "the truthful" and "the trusted" right in his early youth. But the moment he declared the doctrine of Oneness of God and exposed the futility of the pagan idols and statues the Quraish aristocracy became simply furious. They conspired to defame and blackmail him in the vilest possible style. They incited the Makkan masses and miscreants to undo Prophet's widespread public image as a truthful person.

One day when he went out in the streets every one he met on the way labelled him as a liar. He was insulted and ridiculed. Those vile defamatory remarks hurt his heart. He retreated home hurriedly. Covering his body with a mantle he lied down on the bed to heal the trauma of taunts and twits, satires and slanders hurled at him so relentlessly. Then God consoled him by the famous morale—boosting verse: "O you who are enwrapped, rise and warn" (Surah: 74).

Neck Embroiled in Mantle

Here is another display of bad taste. Once while the Prophet was praying in the Kaabah Uqbah b. Mueet felt intrigued to play some dirty tricks on him. He embroiled Prophet's neck in his mantle and then pulled it with a violent jerk. The Prophet fell flat on the ground. Vulgar Uqbah and his wild companions burst into derisive peals of laughters and taunts.

Twisting Prophet's Name

Prophet's name, Muhammad, was as charming as his pious thoughts and lovely deeds. It meant "the praised one", "the laudable", etc. One of the common demoralizing weapon employed by the perverted Makkan pagans was twisting that graceful name. They would address him rudely as Mudhammam which means exactly the opposite, i.e. "reprobate".

But the Prophet ignored all that vulgarity and bad taste with characteristic patience and fortitude. He often used to say: "Aren't you surprised at the injuries from the Quraish which God wards off from me? They curse me and satirize me as Mudhammam, whereas I am Muhammad".

Hurling Camel's Stomach

Once while the Prophet was offering prayers at the Kaabah Abu Jahl and a few other Quraish celebrities assembled around. Abu Jahl said that so and so had slaughtered a camel that day and that its stomach and excreta were still lying in the street. Then he said, "I wish some one went there to fetch the camel's stomach so that I could throw it over Muhammad's neck when he goes into prostration (sajdah)." Upon this Uqbah said, "I will do this service". So the stomach was brought and thrown over Prophet's neck exactly as Abu Jahl had designed.

Rejoicing over that dirty spectacle the pagan vagabonds burst into loud laughters. Meantime some one informed Fatimah about the nasty incident. She was hardly five or six then. She rushed to the spot and removed the stomach and filth from Prophet's body. She rebuked Uqbah for the dirty deed.

Abu Jahl's Vulgarity

One day Abu Jahl chanced to pass by the Prophet near Mount Safa. He taunted the Prophet with his characteristically vile vulgarity and venom. Not satisfied with wild vollies of jeers and jibes he even went to the extent of passing derogatory remarks about Islam. The Prophet, however, demonstrated patience and kept quiet.

Prophet's uncle, Hamza, had gone out for hunting that day. When he returned a female eyewitness told him everything about the insulting episode. Hamza got enraged. He ran out in search of Abu Jahl. Finding him seated and gossiping among a group of his people Hamza hit him with a bow, causing an injury to his head. He then shouted out: "How dare you insult him. Now listen, I too am embracing Islam. Now on I will also say what he says. If you have any guts, treat me too the same way".

Some men got up in support of Abu Jahl. But he stopped them saying: "Let him go for, by God, I too have hurled filthy abuses at his nephew".

The Holy Prophet's boycott deed being hung on Kaabah's walls.

Venomous Deed of Boycott

Quite a few of Prophet's companions had settled successfully in Abyssinia. Some influential Makkan leaders like Umar had come in the folds of Islam. The tribesmen were also embracing Islam in greater number. Prophet Muhammad's noble mission seemed to be propelling forth fairly well. This added to the already mounting fury and frustration of the pagan elite.

Accordingly they held an emergency meeting and decided to propose a plan of boycott on two clans related to the Prophet, Banu Hashim and Banu Muttalib. According to the terms of the boycott a permanent moratorium was placed on contracting marriages and commerical dealings with these two clans and all other Muslims. These points were drafted in the form of a deed of boycott. The venomous deed was then hung up on the wall of Kaabah to remind the Quraish of their cherished obligation of keeping the flames of hatred and hostility afire all the time.

The writer of the historic boycott deed was Mansur b. Ikrima. The Prophet invoked God's displeasure against him and some of his fingers got withered mysteriously.

Slanders and Stones at Taif

When the psychological offensive at Makkah became too grave and unbearable the Prophet thought of disseminating the Divine message at Taif, a town situated at about 90 kilometres towards the east of Makkah. He arrived there on foot and all alone. It was around 619 A.D.

At Taif a group of three brothers, the sons of Amr b. Umayr, enjoyed prestige and power at that time.

A view of the old city of Taif.

The Prophet met each one of the three individually. He invited them to Islam. But they not only refused to accept the invitation but also insulted and ridiculed him badly.

They also turned down Prophet's request to keep the matter secret so that the Makkan tyrants may not be emboldened further against him. They rather incited their slaves, street boys, louts and all sorts of the bad characters of Taif against the Prophet. The infuriated gangs started to chase the Prophet, hurling abuses and stones at him. Then when he was leaving the place in disgust the rascals flanked him on both sides of the street, abusing and stoning him all the way. They chased the badly-bleeding Prophet for quite a long distance.

The Prophet eventually took refuge in a vine orchard and relaxed under the shade of a tree. The owners of the orchard were two good-natured persons, Utba and Shayba. They had witnessed the brutal treatment meted out to the Prophet by the Taif rascals. They were moved by pity and passion for a distressed stranger. They deputed their young Christian slave, Addas, to take a bunch of grapes on a platter to the Prophet. Addas was so impressed by Prophet's talk that he started kissing his head, hands and feet. When his pagan masters saw this they rebuked Addas.

Despite all that rough handling the Prophet was not the least deterred from his noble mission. He returned to Makkah to resume his work there.

She Dashed to Smash Him
Umme Jamil, the notorious wife of a notorious husband, Abu Lahab, used to cast thorns in Prophet's

way. God revealed the following verses about the nasty couple:

The Flame

In the name of God, the Most Gracious,
the Most Merciful

1. Perish the hands of Abu Lahab, and perish he!
2. His wealth avails him not, neither what he has earned.
3. He shall roast at a flaming fire.
4. And his wife, the scandalmongering.
5. Round her neck a rope of palm-fibre.

(*Surah* : 111)

When she heard about these Quranic verses she was simply furious. Picking up a stone she rushed to the mosque where the Prophet was sitting with Abu Bakr. At this critical juncture God made her unable to see the Prophet. So she could see only Abu Bakr. Addressing him she said: "O Abu Bakr, where is your friend? I have been told that he is satirizing me. By God, if I had found him I would have smashed his mouth with this stone. By God, I am a poet." She then recited:

"We reject the reprobate,
His words we repudiate,
His religion we loathe and hate".

When she went away Abu Bakr asked the Prophet in amazement as to why she was not able to see him. The Prophet replied that God had taken her sight away from him.

Tragic Fate of Five Mockers

Those who took sadistic delight in teasing, insulting and mocking the Prophet relentlessly also included some big shots of the town. Five such notorious mockers were: (i) al-Aswad b. al-Muttalib, (ii) al-Aswad b. Abdu Yaguth, (iii) al-Walid b. al-Mughira, (iv) al-Aas b. Wail, and (v) al-Harith b. al-Tulatila.

They were all elderly persons and very well-respected among their clans. They had teased and taunted the Prophet so wildly that about one of them the Prophet had been obliged to utter the curse: "O God, blind him and bereave him of his son".

Then when their mocking and insulting routines reached their climax, God revealed: "Proclaim what you have been ordered and turn away from the polytheists. We will surely protect you against the mockers who put another god besides the God. In the end they will know".

(Surah: 15:94)

Eventually all the five of them met their evil fate. Al-Aswad b. al-Muttalib lost his eye-sight. Al-Aswad b. Abdu Yaguth died of pleurisy. Walid died of an ankle wound. A thorn pierced al-Aas' foot and he died of the fatal wound. The pus discharging from Harith's head wound ended up with his death.

Tempting Traps of Greed and Grandeur

Another unsuccessful weapon tried very frequently by the Quraish aristocracy was the devil of greed and grandeur. The Prophet was severally offered extremely tempting alternatives only if he gave up censoring their gods and the pre-Islamic traditions. In fact, they were quite willing to do just anything for him only if he stopped his guidance programme that was transforming thought and behaviour of the masses, paving thereby the way for the impending Islamic revolution.

Did he desire wealth and riches? They were quite willing to offer him any amount. Was political dominance his ultimate aim? They were not the least hesitant to accept him as their uncontested leader. Was he intending to become a big king? They were willing even to proclaim him as their unchallenged ruler.

Offers of Mental "Treatment"

Some of the pagans really believed and many of them had been induced to think under influence of the powerful propaganda that the Prophet was under some sort of a spell of spirits, jinns, etc. They often addressed him as "majnun" (mad man). Offers were also made to the extent that they could get him treated completely of that spell as well only if he agreed to toe their line.

Death-Wishing for the Prophet

To live and to preach peacefully the Prophet was compelled to migrate to Madina. The bitter psychological offensive, however, continued vexing him even there. At Madina the Jewish offensive was the bitterest. Jews of Madina opposed the Prophet tooth and nail. Whenever they saw him they greeted him jeeringly with the vicious words, "death to you" (assamo alaikum), by making a cunning twist upon the prescribed Islamic words, "peace upon you" (asslamo alaikum).

The Jewish offensive was bitter, no doubt. It could not, however, rival the earlier psychological torture perpetrated on the Prophet by the furious pagans of Makkah. Despite all that torture and maltreatment the Prophet never wavered in pursuing his noble mission. He continued to proclaim what God had ordered him to. He rather became more and more active in demonstrating the futility of the pagan gods and goddesses, their unhealthy way of life and their rampant moral lewdness.

All sorts of luring offers and frightening postures from the pagans failed to work. The Holy Prophet continued his enlightening mission with unfailing vigour and enthusiasm. In fact one of the Prophet's answers to Quraish's luring offers stands as a unique masterpiece of a committed missionary's refusal to compromise on principles. He said: "If the Quraish place the sun on one of my hands and the moon on the other even then I will not give up my mission. I will fulfil my mission or lay down my life for it".

Convinced of the collapse of their psychological offensives the Quraish became more and more dismayed. Hurt to the core they grew more bitter, more wicked, more violent and more desperate.

QUESTIONS

1. What did the pagans of Makkah do to defame the Holy Prophet?
2. What vulgar trick did Uqbah play on the Prophet while he was praying in Kaabah?
3. How was Prophet's name twisted by the pagans?
4. Describe the incident of the throwing of camel's stomach on the Prophet.
5. How did Abu Jahl misbehave with the Prophet?
6. What was the Deed of Boycott against the Muslims?
7. How was the Prophet insulted and manhandled at Taif?

8. What did Umme Jamil do when she heard of the revelation of the Surah Lahab?
9. How did the five mockers meet their tragic fate?
10. What traps of greed and grandeur were laid against the Prophet?
11. Why did the Quraish make an offer for mental "treatment" to the Prophet?
12. How did the Jews of Madina wish death for the Prophet?

9

MURDEROUS ATTEMPTS ON PROPHET'S LIFE

The psychological offensives were reinforced by a diversity of assassination attempts on Prophet's life. These abortive bids to kill range from sporadic ill-planned assaults to shrewdly-designed individual and collective plots and plans of a really horrendous magnitude. That the Holy Prophet escaped all those death traps looks like a great miracle indeed. In the whole history of human race Prophet's personality stands out as a unique case of a benevolent being who was so hotly pursued by so vicious a progeny of ruthless rascals and who had a narrow escape each time. The main weapons relied by the conspiring murderers were heavy stones, sharp swords and deadly poisons. The details of all such murderous assaults attempted at various times and places have been presented here in one place.

First Attempt on Life

The first attempt on his life was made at Makkah at a time when the total number of the Muslims was about forty. It happened on the day the Prophet publicly declared the unity of God in the very precincts of the Kaabah. He told the people that it was a futile ritual to worship man-made idols and statues. A group of Makkan pagans then fell upon him. One of the Prophet's companions, Harith b. Abi Hala, lost his life while defending the Prophet. This was the first blood ever shed in the way of God.

Gang Attack and Narrow Escape

Since quite a long time the Quraish had been feeling rather bitterly that Muhammad had rendered them inestimable harm. He had declared their mode of life foolish, insulted their forefathers, reviled their religion, cursed their gods and divided their community. Their emotional pain was becoming increasingly unbearable. They were desperate and on the look out for an adequate opportunity to settle accounts with him.

One day, while the Prophet was performing tawaf at the Kaabah some miscreants levelled slanderous allegations against him. When this was repeated thrice the Prophet stopped and said: "will you listen to me, O Quraish? By Him Who holds my life in His hand I will murder and finish you". This rather unusual utterance from Prophet's mouth so struck those reckless rascals that they got nonplussed. Standing silent, they stopped insulting him. Even the most tough of the gang adopted a meak and respecting posture, saying: "Depart, O Abu 'l-Qasim, for, by God, you are not violent!" On this the Prophet resumed his tawaf.

Next morning the ruffians assembled near the Black Stone in the Kaabah. They started to review the past episode. They wondered how they let the Prophet go after having heard so much of the unpleasant threats. While they were busy reviewing the episode the Prophet chanced to appear on the scene. They leaped upon him. Encircling him on all sides they yelled: "Are you the one who said so and so against our gods and our religion?" The Prophet replied promptly: "Yes I am indeed the one who said so". On hearing this the gang got furious and fell upon him. One of them even seized Prophet's robe from the front.

The matter was about to take a more serious turn. Suddenly Abu Bakr appeared on the scene and interposed himself. With tearful eyes he shouted: "May God destroy you, would you kill a man who says Allah is my Lord?" On this the rogues left the Prophet and fell upon Abu Bakr. He was a hairy man. They dragged him along by his beard. The hair of his head was badly pulled and torn. When he returned home that day he was having a severe headache.

Abu Jahl's Stoning Plot

Once Abu Jahl incited a Quraish gathering in Makkah against the Prophet. He said that the Prophet had insulted the Arab religion, culture and people. He further declared that he had intended to pick up the biggest available stone and to sit in hiding for the Prophet. As soon as he went in prostration during the prayer he had determined to crush his head with the stone. He said he did not care whether or not people sided him after the assassination.

The next morning Abu Jahl actually got hold of a huge stone and sat close to the Prophet while he was praying. As soon as the prophet prostrated he dashed at him. Approaching near him he, however, retracted his steps suddenly with a queer emotional state. Whole of his body was shivering. His face had darkened. He looked simply horror-stricken. Both of his hands seemed jammed over the huge stone that he was carrying. He retraced his steps and threw it away abruptly.

This unusual behaviour on Abu Jahl's part astonished the Quraish group standing nearby and waiting anxiously for the outcome of the much-bragged of stoning bravado. On being questioned by his people to explain the mystery, Abu Jahl reported: "I stood by his side to do that which I had mentioned you about last night. When I came close to him a camel stood between me and him. By God, I have never seen a camel of that size and stature, nor any neck of that type, nor the teeth of that nature in any camel. That frightful camel was about to devour me."

Later when the Prophet was asked about the "camel" in Abu Jahl's narration he said: "It was Gibraeel. Had he come near it, it would have got hold of him".

Umar Rushes to Murder

During the pre-Islamic days even Umar had once planned to murder the Prophet. He was hyper-aggressive by temperament. Annoyed with growing popularity of Islam he decided to assassinate the Prophet. Armed with a sharp sword he was proceeding towards the Prophet's house in an angry mood when Naeem b. Abdullah met him on the way. Finding him looking rather upset he enquired about his intentions. Umar

70

replied that he was going to put an end to the Prophet. Naeem informed him that his own sister and brother-in-law too had embraced Islam and that he should take care of them first.

Changing his course the enraged Umar then hastened straight to his sister's house. It was there that he got the opportunity of listening to some Quranic Verses which changed his entire destiny. It then so happened that a fiery Umar, who just a few moments back was mad with the intent to murder the Prophet, was then seen speeding towards the same direction with an entirely changed outlook. At that moment the Prophet was at a companion's house near Mount Safa. With his sword still hanging by his side Umar appeared before him and embraced Islam to the thundering applause of Allah-o-Akbar by everyone, including the Prophet himself.

Murder After House Blockade

When most of Prophet's companions had left for Madina he was still staying at Makkah waiting for the Divine permission to migrate. Of his main supporters only Abu Bakr and Ali were left at Makkah.

Realizing that the Prophet was gaining popularity despite their opposition and offensives the Quraish aristocrats had turned more bitter and more violent. In utter desperation they convened a big assembly of chosen chiefs. They mooted to draft a decisive action plan to handle the Prophet properly. Three main proposals came under discussion in that historic session:

   (i) life imprisonment in shackles,
   (ii) disposal through exile, and
   (iii) instant assassination.

The last-mentioned proposal was presented by the master brain, Abu Jahl. All the furious Quraish chiefs unanimously approved Abu Jahl's proposal. It was decided to impose a complete blockade over Prophet's house so that he could not run away. A strong contingent of tough guards was, accordingly, posted outside the house. They were to assassinate him forthwith while he lay asleep that night or came out for the morning prayers.

That dreadful night the Prophet asked Ali under Divine guidance to sleep on his bed, covering his body with his mantle. While the Prophet slipped away from the back door the Quraish guards thought that he lay asleep in his bed with his mantle on. The Prophet then stayed in the Thaur Cave for three days along with his close companion, Abu Bakr. On the fourth day they set out for Madina on camel backs. The Quraish were furious to learn that the Prophet had escaped the death trap. They immediately announced a luring reward of one hundred she-camels for his arrest. Despite several horse-riders pursuing them hotly the Prophet and his companion managed to reach Madina quite safe and sound.

Murder with Poisoned Sword

Umayr b. Wahb and Safwan b. Ummayyah, two Makkan pagans used to feel unusually depressed after the Badr debacle. Umayr's son was a prisoner of war with Muslims at Madina. Safwan had lost his father in the Badr Battle. One day both of them conspired to meet in a deserted place in the outskirts of Makkah. They explored together ways and means of murdering the Prophet. Said Safwan, "By God, life has now lost all its charm for me." "You are right", remarked Umayr. "If I had no outstanding debts to pay I would have dashed to Madina to murder Muhammad. My son is in prison there." On this Safwan said, "don't bother about your debts and children. I will look after them. You just go ahead with your task."

Umayr hastened to his home and picked up his sword. He sharpened it and soaked it with poison. Riding a camel he dashed towards Madina. While his camel was kneeling down near Prophet's Mosque Umar chanced to see him. Suspecting his dubious looks he snatched his poisoned sword. Gripping him by the neck he dragged him to the Prophet. The Prophet asked Umar to leave Umayr alone. Then addressing Umayr he said, "come closer to me. What brings you here?" Umayr replied, "I have come to see my son." The Prophet remarked, "why were you armed with a sword? Did n't you and Safwan hatch a conspiracy to kill me while you were sitting at such and such a deserted place outside Makkah? You have now come here with that very evil intent. But you have failed to realize that I am protected by God".

Umayr was simply spellbound. He said, "Muhammad, you are undoubtedly a Divine messenger. By God none but me and Safwan knew about the conspiracy". Saying this he accepted Islam.

Assassination Attempts at Uhud
Although the Battle of Uhud was a clash between the forces of good and evil, it appeared as if the major and almost the sole, target of the enemy was consistently one and the same – assassinating the Prophet.

During this battle Prophet's companion, Musaab

b. Umayr, who resembled him most, was martyred by Ibn Qamia, a stalwart of the Quraish. After the killing Ibn Qamia returned to his people and reported, "I have killed Muhammad". At this the rumour began to spread like wild fire that the Prophet had been assassinated. This created an unprecedented panic and depression in the Muslim camp. They got so badly demoralized that even Umar threw away his sword in grief and despair.

The first man who found that the Prophet was alive was Kaab b. Malik. Kaab said, "I recognized his bright eyes gleaning from beneath his helmet. I called out at the top of my voice: "Take heart O Muslims, the Apostle of God is here". This revived the morale in the Muslim camp. They began to put in a tough resistance thereafter.

At one stage during the battle Ibn Qamia came too close to the Prophet. He thrust his sword over his face. The Prophet's face was badly injured and he lost four of his teeth. Even while he was surrounded on all sides by the invading enemies he was repeatedly praying: "O Lord, forgive my people, they don't know".

The battle was over soon. The forces of Quraish failed this time too in their long-cherished desire to kill the Prophet.

"Who Will Save You?"

Once while returning from a battle in the Najd territory the Prophet and his companions decided to have some siesta at a place on the way where a number of trees were growing. The companions went to rest underneath a groove. They fell asleep soon. The Prophet selected a nearby acacia tree for the siesta. Hanging his sword on a branch of the tree he too fell asleep.

In the meantime considering it an ideal opportunity to put an end to the Prophet a bedouin, Ghaurath b. al-Harith, got hold of the hanging sword and leapt upon him shouting: "Who will save you from me now?" The Prophet, who by then had woken up, replied: "Allah alone". Over-awed by the grace and simplicity of the forthright answer the bedouin began to shiver. The sword slipped from his hand. The Prophet picked it up quickly, saying: "Who will save you from me now?" The confused bedouin had nothing to say. But the Prophet pardoned him. Finding the Prophet extending such a generous treatment even to a manifest foe the bedouin embraced Islam there and then.

The Prophet then woke up his sleeping companions. He narrated them the entire story in the presence of the unsuccessful murderer.

The Stone—Throwing Conspiracy

One day during 4 A.H. the Prophet went to Banu Nuzayr, the notorious Jewish tribe. They made him sit and wait besides a ditch. They then hatched a plan to throw a huge grinding stone over him from the roof of the adjoining house while he sat there. Amr b. Hajjash, who was deputed to throw the stone, climbed up the roof to do the needful. The Prophet, however, sensed their evil design. He left the place in time under the pretext of going out to answer the call of nature.

The "Feast" to Kill

The famous Jewish leader Kaab b. Ashraf, was renowned for his wealth, power and poetry. He nursed a lava of hatred against Islam. Once he arranged a fake "feast" in honour of the Prophet. He commissioned a few miscreants to put an end to Prophet's life as soon as he arrived for the feast. This murder bid also failed.

Death During "Discussion"

The Jewish tribe of Banu Nuzayr once sent a message to the Prophet inviting him to come for a "discussion" along with three men. He was asked to elaborate his viewpoint. They assured him that if their religious scholars, the rabbis, were convinced by the Prophet they would embrace Islam. The Prophet accepted the invitation. But while he was still on the way he received information that the inviting Jews had armed themselves fully. They were sitting in wait to murder him on arrival for the pretended "discussion". The Prophet retreated immediately.

Twelve Masked Desperadoes

Once a gang of twelve hardened rogues conspired to kill the Prophet. At a secret meeting wherein the nefarious plot was hatched, highly inflammable speeches were delivered. Jallas said. "we are being treated as sheep and Muslims have become our shepherds. We are idiots and they alone are the wise…. If this man (the Prophet) is on the right then we are even worse than the asses." Advising the conspirators Abdullah b. Ubbay, the notorious hypocrite, said: "If you keep awake tonight you will be safe for ever. You have no other option but to kill the man today".

So this gang of twelve desperadoes determined to kill the Prophet in the darkness of the night while he was to pass through Aqbah. The conspirators were wearing masks. The Prophet, however, had already been alerted through a Divine sign. He managed to escape unhurt. During their scuffle with one of the Prophet's companions the masked conspirators were identified. Frightened by the consequences of detection they fled away and got mixed up in a nearby crowd.

The next morning the Prophet summoned them. He interrogated each one of them about the nightly episode. Each one gave his own rationalized defence. Despite the gravity of their offence and confession of the guilt the Prophet pardoned all of them.

Killing During "Conversation"

Once a deputation of Bani Amer waited on the Prophet at Madina. The deputation included a number of rascals and dare-devils. Of these Amer b. Tufail and Arbad b. Qais had hatched a plot to assassinate the Prophet. It was agreed that while Amer was to engage the Prophet in a deceptive conversation Arbad was to attack and kill him with a sword.

Having settled everything both the rascals came near the Prophet. Amer said, "O Muhammad, I desire to talk to you in seclusion". The Prophet replied, "I can't accede to your request until you accept Islam". Amer went on repeating the request for several times, waiting for Arbad to attack the Prophet. Arbad, however, sat unmoved. Seeing this Amer repeated his request finally. When the Prophet gave the same answer Amer threatened him saying: "All right, I will now bring such a powerful army of red horsemen and infantrymen that the whole of Madina will be filled with them".

When Amer left after the threat the Prophet said, "O God, take care of Amer b. Tufail". After leaving the Prophet Amer asked Arbad as to why he did not attack the Prophet as settled between them, adding, "by God, I consider you the most coward man on earth. Now on I will have nothing to do with you". On this Arbad replied: "Don't be hasty. Listen to me too. By God, when I intended to comply with your wishes I found you standing between me and him. I could see none but you. Should I have attacked you then?".

The two ruffians then left Madina for their native place. While still on the way Amer got afflicted with plague. A tumour appeared on his neck. He breathed his last at the residence of a woman of Bani Salool tribe. After his burial Arbad reached home. His people enquired from him as to what had happened. Arbad replied, "nothing, by God, Muhammad asked us to worship something which, if I get hold of, I would kill it with my arrow". A day or two afterwards he set out to sell his camel. But while on the way lightening struck him hard. He and his camel were reduced to ashes.

The Poisoned Roast Drama

On the occasion of the conquest of Khaybar a wicked Jewish woman, Zainab d. al-Harith, prepared a roasted lamb for the Prophet. She mixed poison in the meat. On ascertaining from the Prophet that he had a special liking for lamb's forearm she mixed excessive dosage of a more deadly brand of the poison in that particular part of the roast.

She then took the poisoned roast meat to the

Prophet and presented it to him as a food gift. As the Prophet took a bite of the meat he threw it out of his mouth at once saying, "the meat tells me that there is poison in it." He prohibited his companions too to eat the poisoned stuff. One of his companions, Bashr b. Bra, was amongst those present in that meeting. He had also tasted a slice of the poisoned meat. Although he too had felt bitterness of the poison he did not deem it appropriate to spit it out in the presence of the Holy Prophet. Accordingly, the morsel slipped down his throat. The poisoning process that had started ended up with his death later on.

The Jewish woman was summoned by the Prophet. She confessed the crime and disclosed that a number of other Jews had also been working actively behind the poisoning plot. On being interrogated those background conspirators also confessed their complicity in the plot. The great Prophet, however, pardoned the cunning woman and all her accomplices.

Murderous Assault During Tawaf

After conquest of Makkah the Prophet stayed in the city for sometime. Once during those days while he was busy in the Tawaf of the Holy Kaabah Fazala b. Ummayr chased him quietly and sneaked into the Kaabah. He sat in ambush with the intent to assassinate him. He was about to make the final assault when the Prophet moved close to him and told him all about his secret designs.

Fazala got nervous over the unexpected exposure of his evil intentions. As he felt quite ashamed of his dirty plot the Prophet placed his hand affectionately over him. He asked him to repent to God. Such an unusually kind treatment changed Fazala's mental outlook altogether. He repented and embraced Islam.

"I'ill Finish Him Today"

During the Uhud Battle Shaibah b. Uthman's father had been killed at the hands of the Muslims. Since that day he had been burning badly in the fire of revenge. During the Conquest of Makkah one day he happened to see the Prophet and his followers from a close distance. The flames of retaliation got enkindled with added fury. Unable to control his fiery passions he hastened to announce publicly that he would kill the Prophet that day. He then started to circle round the Prophet in a furious manner, in a desperate bid to find an appropriate opportunity to deliver the fatal blow.

As he was so engaged in circling round he suddenly felt as if some invisible object had stood in between him and the Prophet. That unseen object appeared to exert against him with full force. Shaibah paused and stood dazed. The ensuing mental state extinguished all his revengeful flames. He realized too soon that some invisible power was protecting the Prophet from the evil design he had hatched against him.

QUESTIONS

1. When was the first attempt made to murder the Prophet?
2. What happened to Abu Bakr when he tried to protect the Prophet from the gangsters?
3. Why did Abu Jahl's attempt to stone the Prophet to death fail?
4. What happened when Umar left his house to murder the Prophet?
5. Describe briefly the plot to assassinate the Prophet after bloc-

kading his house.

6. How did Umayr fail to kill the Prophet with the poisoned sword?
7. What led to the rumour of Prophet's death at Uhud?
8. How did the bedouin try to kill the Prophet during noon nap under the tree?
9. How did the Prophet escape the Jewish plot to murder him by stone-throw from a roof top?
10. How did Kaab conspire to kill the Prophet during a fake "feast"?
11. How did the Jews plot to murder the Prophet during a fake "discussion"?
12. What was the murder plot of the twele masked desperadoes?
13. How did the two rascals conspire to kill the Prophet during a deceptive "conversation"?
14. Describe the poisoned roast meat plot hatched by the wicked Jewish woman?
15. Describe Fazala's unsuccessful bid to murder the Prophet during the tawaf.
16. What happened to Shaibah when he circled round the Prophet to kill him?

10

BEWITCHING THE PROPHET WITH BLACK MAGIC

The Jewish lobby and the Pagan forces of Arabia were badly after the Prophet. They did not spare even the age-old weapon of black magic and witchcraft in their desperate bid to demoralize, incapacitate, bewilder and kill the Holy Prophet. So ruthlessly vicious and vengeful was indeed the psyche of those stubborn people.

Knotted Cord and Needled Effigy

Labid b. Asim was a renowned magician of ancient Arabia. Being either a Jew or a hypocrite he had cordial relations with the Jews of Madina. Once around 7 A.H. a deputation of Jews from Khaybar visited Madina. Calling on Labid they narrated concocted accounts of Prophet's alleged maltreatment of the Jewish community. Exaggerated tales of their woes and worries were played up. They told him that they had tried in vain a diversity of magical devices and witchcraft tactics against the Prophet. They were sure

The magic cord with eleven knots as recovered from the Zarwan well.

that a master mind like him alone could help them in the hour of their frustration and dismay. Offering three guineas for the job they requested him to accept the fee and to devise and play a specially-powerful magic on the Prophet. Greed of money and flames of hatred gripped Labid's mind. He consented to render the requisite professional services.

During those days a good-natured Jewish boy had been so impressed by Prophet's life style and teachings that he had joined his personal service. The conspiring gang prevailed upon that young servant to obtain a piece of Prophet's comb with some of his head's hair stuck over it. Labid subjected the hair and the comb to a special magical process. According to a variant narration he got the magical ritual effected by his sisters who had a better command over primitive magic and witchcraft. The spelled comb and hair were then covered in the spike of a male date-palm. The choice of the cover was determined by the fact that the male palm resembles the colour of male skin. Labid then hid the material underneath a rock at the bottom of Zarwan well in accordance with a meticulously-prescribed magical device. Along with the above-mentioned material there were two other items which were also buried at the same place: (i) a magic string with eleven knots tied in it, and (ii) a wax effigy of the Prophet with needles pierced all over.

Disturbances in Prophet's Personal Life

Although Prophet's Divine functioning as God's messenger was not the least impaired by the evil magic, his personal life did appear to be affected considerably. The impact of the magic process took about one year to gain full momentum. He had begun to experience a queer psychophysical state. After six months some change in temperament started to be felt.

With the passage of time the pernicious impact intensified quite a bit. The last forty days of the spell were painful. He had been turning lean and pale day by day without a plausible cause. His personal memory seemed to be fading. On several occasions he would think that he had completed a personal piece of work even though he had not yet touched it. He often doubted his own visual process. Sometimes he imagined having seen something whereas the facts pointed to the contrary. His routine life also appeared affected. He would think that he had seen some people without actually having seen them.

It is recorded in history that the operational sphere of this irritating state was exclusively confined to his private life. It did not the least affect his functioning as an Apostle. There is not even a distant reference available to the effect that during the period of the magic spell the Prophet forgot a Quranic verse or misquoted the same. No change was visible in his mosque sermons, public addresses and guidance sessions. He led all prayers with his characteristic enthusiasm and usual regularity. Had there been a slight change or even a minor lapse in the Divinely-ordained functioning of Prophet's office there would have been an uproar of unending hostile criticism and bitter propaganda. As a matter of fact the unpleasant impact of the magic was so strictly personal and selective that the general mass of the people were totally unaware of what was happening to the person of the Prophet. Nevertheless, the magic spell had become a source of virtual annoyance and immense inconvenience to him, his family and close friends. In fact, the pangs of the spell had intensified during the last three days.

How the Magic Was Nullified?

Once when Prophet's anguish under the magic spell was severe he prayed to God repeatedly for a speedy recovery. As he lay half-asleep and drowsy in that state two angels appeared before him in human garb. One stood towards the head-side of the cot and the other towards the feet-side. In the form of a mutual dialogue they apprised the Prophet of the details of the mechanism and mystery of Labid's magical device.

The Prophet then hastened to depute a team of five Muslims to the Zarwan well. The group comprised of Ali, Ammar, Zubayr, Jubayr and Qais. After a short while he also arrived at the spot in the company of some friends. Soon the process of undoing the back magic went into full operation. It was found that the water of the well had turned red like the leaves of henna tree. The entire water was drained out of the well. The palm cover containing Prophet's hair and comb was retrieved from underneath the rock. They also traced out the cord with eleven knots and the needle-studded wax effigy.

Recitation of Anti-Magic Panacea

At this stage angel Gibraeel appeared on the scene and advised the Prophet to recite the last two Surahs of the Holy Quran: (i) al-Falaq (Dawn: 113), and (ii) an-Nas (Mankind: 114). It may be noted that the first Surah is composed of five verses and the second of six. The verses in both the Surahs thus total eleven. It may be remembered that the number of the knots on the magic cord was also eleven. Both the Surahs, taken together, are known as Muawwidhatain ('the two Surahs seeking Divine refuge'). Full English texts of the Muawwidhatain are given below:

(1) The Dawn (al-Falaq)
In the name of Allah, the Beneficent, the Merciful.
  (i)   Say, I seek refuge in the Lord of the Dawn,
 (ii)   From the evil of that which He created,
(iii)   And from the evil of the darkness when it is intense,
 (iv)   And from the evil of the sorceresses who blow on knots,
  (v)   And from the evil of the envier when he envies.

The point warrants special notice that verse number (iv) above literally means: "And from the evil of blowers upon Knots". This is an obvious reference to the common form of witchcraft rampant in pre-Islamic Arabia wherein the magicians, mostly women, used to tie knots in a cord and blow upon them with magical sayings.

(2) The Mankind (an-Nas)
In the name of Allah, the Beneficent, the Merciful.
  (i)   Say, I seek refuge in the Lord of mankind,
 (ii)   The King of mankind,
(iii)   The God of mankind,
 (iv)   From the evil of sneaking whisperer,

   (v) Who whispers in the hearts of mankind,
   (vi) From the Jinns and the mankind.

The Prophet Feels Unshackled

As the Prophet went on reciting one verse after the other, knots after knots of the magic cord began to be unfolded and needles after needles of the wax effigy extracted out. At the completion of the entire recital of eleven verses of the Muawwidhatain all the eleven knots of the magic cord had been undone and all the needles of the wax effigy extracted. With the unfastening of each knot of the cord and the extraction of each needle of the effigy the Prophet went on feeling better and better. When the process reached its end the Prophet came out of the magic spell completely. He reported that he felt as if a chained person had been unshackled. The painful spell had lasted about one year.

After his emancipation from the magic spell the Prophet summoned Labid and asked for his explanation. He confessed his misdeed. The Prophet, however, pardoned him saying that it was an episode taking place in the orbit of his personal life and that he did not deem it advisable to take any disciplinary action. He even prohibited publicity of the magic episode so that none of his followers be incited to pick up arms in revenge. As a matter of fact some of his infuriated companions had intended to murder the wicked magician but the Prophet pacified them by saying: "God has granted me convalescence. I don't intend enkindling strife among people for my own self".

Magic and its Impact on Prophets

The all-too intriguing magic issue has been a subject of considerable controversy among Muslim and non-Muslim scholars. Islam acknowledges the existence and operation of magic and witchcraft as an evil reality. However, its practice is strictly forbidden as is the practice of all other evil media meant to harm human mind and body. The Holy Quran holds magic as disbelief ('kufr') obviously because it is an evil system, seeking the support of satans, spirits and stars for the purpose of damaging mankind. It is reported in Bukhari and Muslim on the authority of Abu Hurairah that the seven deadly sins identified by the Prophet include magic at serial order two in his list. Several other traditions support and supplement this viewpoint.

The basic issue here is: Can Prophets be influenced by magical processes? One school of thought gives the answer in a categorical no. In the history of Islam the Mu'tazilites and the Modernists have rejected the entire magic episode as a fabrication and a concoction. The grounds of denial are that the world of magic and witchcraft are not amenable to human logic and perception and that Prophets could never be bewitched.

The other school of thought, however, takes the stand that even a Prophet, after all, is a human being. If life's exigencies, bodily wounds, poisonous stuffs, wild animals and emotional traumas can affect his being then his psychophysical make-up could as well be temporarily influenced by other powerful extraneous forces like slanderous offensives, magic exercises and the like. Previous precedent of Prophet Musa (pbuh) is there to support the thesis. It is a historical fact that he was, in fact, impressed somewhat by the enchanting performance of Firaun's royal magicians.

Furthermore, magic's adverse impact on human mind has also been aptly alluded to in the Surah al-Baqarah.

A Factual Historical Episode

In order to construe a correct picture of the issue in its precise perspective the actual facts warrant a clear focus. Labid's magic had a temporary effect on Prophet's personal life stream. Needless to reemphasize that his life and office as a Divine messenger continued to remain intact. He continued to perform all those functions smoothly without the least interruption or interference by the magic episode. The Muslim historians happened to be the founders of objective narration. They have faithfully reported interesting details of an historical event exactly as it happened in time and space. They could as well have opted to delete or distort this otherwise unpleasant episode from all Seerat narrations. This rather unusual episode too has found factual mention in all authentic Seerat literature.

The narration, therefore warrants credence in the form in which it has been transmitted to posterity. There may be some people who are still unable to appreciate the metaphysical mysteries of this apparently-incredible incident. Such persons could reconcile to the blunt reality that human life continues to be replete with infinite events and episodes which are not yet normally amenable to ordinary logic or reason. Many a facet of human life on this wonderful planet have been, are even now and shall continue to be shrouded in a mist of mystery.

Whatever the case one thing stands out crystal clear. The inhumane anti-Islamic forces of the day had spared no stone unturned to pervert, pollute and perish the mind and body of the great Prophet in a desperate bid to flop his life-giving mission.

QUESTIONS

1. How did the Jews of Madina persuade Labid to play magic on the Prophet?
2. What role did the Prophet's Jewish servant play in the evil game?
3. What magic materials were concealed at the bottom of Zarwan well?
4. What was the effect of the magic on Prophet's personal life?
5. How was the magic nullified?
6. How did the Prophet feel when the magic spell was undone?
7. Why have the Muslim historians recorded the magic episode?

11

MUHAMMAD MIGRATES TO MADINA

Some of Prophet's companions had left for Madina while he stayed in Makkah waiting for Divine permission to migrate. Of his major supporters only Abu Bakr and Ali were left at Makkah. The two other categories of people who were forced to stay on were:

(i) those who were under some sort of a restraint, and

(ii) those who had been forced to renounce Islam.

Conspiracy in the Town Hall

The Prophet was gaining popularity despite stiffening opposition and mounting offensives from the Quraish aristocrats. They had consequently become more apprehensive, more ruthless and more aggressive. They then assembled in Qusayy b. Kilab's house, which was their council chamber. In that town hall all their important affairs used to be reviewed. There they mooted to prepare a decisive action plan about the Prophet. That very day, called al-Zahma, the devil also called on them in the garb of a handsome old man.

He was wearing a coarse mantle. He stood at the door of the council chamber. On being questioned about his identity the devil told them that he was a Shaikh from the highlands. Having heard of the meeting he had come to participate and, possibly, to offer them some useful advice. He was allowed entry.

Top ranking leaders of the Quraish, including the master brain, Abu Jahl, had assembled at that historic meeting. Some representatives from other clans had also been invited. The discussion opened with the preamble that Muhammad had assumed the magnitude of a grave threat to the survival and solidarity of the Quraish. The delegates were told that the meeting had been specially-convened to determine the best course to be pursued to dispose him off.

Imprisonment, Exile and Murder Models

As the furious Quraish chiefs mooted the issue under the guidance of the disguised devil three deadly proposals to get rid of the Prophet came under limelight. They were:

(1) Life imprisonment in shackles,
(2) Disposal through exile, and
(3) Instant assassination.

The exponent of the imprisonment plan proposed to shackle the Prophet and then put him behind the bars. The mover said that by so handling the Prophet same ill-fate would befall him as had fallen to the lot of the two poets, Zuhayr and Nabigha and others. To this the devil in Shaikh's disguise objected on the ground that when the news of imprisonment would leak out his devoted followers were sure to strike and retrieve their loving Prophet. In fact, he told them that being unsound the proposed measure might even destroy altogether the authority of the Quraish. The imprisonment proposal was accordingly abandoned.

The propounder of the second proposal suggested to drive the Prophet out of the country. Once he was out of sight they would feel relieved, he argued. They would then endeavour to restore the shattered fabric of their sociocultural life to its pre-Islamic stature. The Shaikh objected to this plan too. He said it was not a sound proposal on the ground that Prophet's charismatic personality, impressive speech, effective diction and compelling force of his message were so luring that wherever he might settle he was sure to muster supporters and devotees around him. They might then invade the Quraish, rob them of their position and trample their authority. "Drop the exile idea", advised the disguised Satan, "and think of a better plan".

Devil Favours Prophet's Assassination

At this Abu Jahl took the floor. He said he had conceived of a plan which had not been hatchd before. Spelling out details of his vicious plot to assassinate the Prophet he said that each clan was to select one young and stout warrior of an aristocratic heritage. The selected warriors were to be armed with sharp swords. Then each one of them was to strike a piercing blow at the Prophet simultaneously, putting an end to him rather instantaneously. The responsibility of the proposed murder would thus lie not upon one particular individual or tribe only but on all the clans jointly. The Muslims could not possibly fight against all of them. They would thus be compelled to accept the bloodmoney which, Abu Jahl said, they would all contribte to pay.

There was a glee of relief and joy on the face of the devil Shaikh. He exclaimed, "the man is right. In my opinion it is the only right thing to do". The proposal to assassinate the Holy Prophet through a collective venture was thus unanimously approved. The meeting was adjourned. The participants then dispersed with a sense of satisfaction and relief.

God Guides the Prophet

The devilish brains of the ferocious Quraish then busied themselves working out further details. Soon the *modus operandi* of the proposed assassination plot was finalized. At this critical juncture angel Gibraeel visited the Prophet and said, "don't sleep tonight on the bed on which you usually sleep."

During late night the group of selected rogues and rascals surrounded Prophet's house. They waited for him to go to bed so that they might attack him while he was asleep or pounce upon him when he came out for the morning prayer. On sensing the grimness of the situation the Prophet instructed Ali to wrap himself up in his green Hadrami mantle in which he usually enwrapped himself while going to bed. He assured Ali that no harm would befall him.

Then Abu Jahl appeared on the scene. Addressing the commandos in a combustible tone he told them: "Muhammad claims that if you follow him you will be Kings of the Arabs and the Persians. Then after death you will be raised to gardens like those of the Jordan. But if you do not follow him you will be slaughtered. And when you are raised from the dead you will burn in the fire of Hell." At this the Prophet

Abu Jahl's armed ruffians besieging Holy Prophet's house.

opened the door and came out with a handful of dust saying: "I do say so. You are one of them."

When Enemy Failed to See

It so happened that God took away their sight. Flabbergasted utterly, they could not see him. The Prophet began to sprinkle the dust over their heads as he recited the Quranic verses: "O man, by the wise Quran. Surely you are one of the messengers, on a right path. A revelation from the Mighty and the Merciful that you may warn a people whose fore-fathers were not warned, they are, therefore, heedless. The sentence is surely justified against most of them, for they do not believe. Surely We will place on their necks iron collars coming up to their chins, so they have their heads raised aloft. And We shall set a barrier before them and a barrier behind them, and cover them over so that they will not be able to see". (Surah 36: 1−9). When he finished each one of the rascals had dust on his head.

After this the Prophet left the place all unnoticed. Then someone from the conspirators came to the stupefied miscreants. He asked them what they were waiting for there. On their reply that they were waiting for Muhammad he said furiously, "Good heavens, Muhammad came out to you, threw dust on your heads and then went away. Can't you see what has happened to you?" Touching their heads with hands they felt the dust sprinkled all over their hair. They then forced entry into the sieged house and began to make a thorough search. Someone was lying on Prophet's bed, all wrapped up in his mantle. Mistaking him for the Prophet they said: "By God, it is Muhammad sleeping with his mantle on." They thus remained under the spell of that mistaken notion until the next morning when Ali got up from the bed. Seeing Ali instead of the Prophet emerging out of the mantle they realized that they had been outwitted. They were furious. As Ali was too young they spared him after giving a reprimand.

The verses which were revealed about that memorable day and the unsuccessful assassination plot read thus: "Remember, when the disbelievers conspired to make you a prisoner or to murder you or to expel you, they plotted, but God also planned; and God's plan is the best." (*Surah* 8:30).

It was only at this critical stage that God granted the Prophet permission to migrate to Madina. When the Prophet allowed Abu Bakr to accompany him he wept with joy. Abu Bakr had purchased two camels which he had held in readiness elsewhere for their intended ride to Madina. The departure was kept in secrecy. None except Ali and Abu Bakr's family knew about it. The Prophet directed Ali to stay behind in Makkah in order to return goods to their owners which people had deposited with the Prophet as trusts. Despite all opposition to him the Makkans knew full well that there was none else as honest and as trustworthy as Prophet Muhammad.

Hiding in Thaur Cave

When the Prophet decided to embark upon the hazardous journey he came quietly to Abu Bakr's house. The two great friends stepped out softly by a window at the back of the house. They set out swiftly towards the Thaur Cave on the Makkan mountains.

Before their departure Abu Bakr had finalized the following arrangements:

(1) he commissioned his son, Abdullah, to listen to the public talk carefully and to visit them at the cave each night with the report of daily events;

(2) he asked his freedman, Amir b. Fuhayra, to graze his flock of sheep along with the Makkan shepherds during the day and to bring it back to them in the cave at night for a regular supply of milk and mutton; and

(3) he instructed his young daughter, Asma, to fetch them food each night.

The Prophet had no shoes on his feet. The sharp loose stones lying scattered on the mountain path made deep cuts in his naked feet. Abu Bakr, therefore, carried him on his back up to the mouth of the cave. The two of them had planned to take a temporary refuge inside the cave till the fury of the pursuing rascals subsided. Before entering the Thaur Cave on the first night Abu Bakr stepped in first to ensure if any snake or wild beast was hiding inside. The Prophet and his faithful friend stayed in the cave for three days.

Some chasers even managed to reach up to the mouth of the cave. When Abu Bakr heard the sound of their footsteps he showed anxiety. The Prophet consoled him saying, "don't worry, God is certainly with us." As a matter of fact nature was helping them all along. A spider had spun a web at the mouth of the cave. A wild dove had built a nest outside the cave and laid eggs. So when the chasing Quraish saw the web and the nest they were convinced that the Prophet

The cobweb and the dove-nest outside the Thaur Cave bamboozled
the chasing pagans.

could not be hiding in such a desolate place. They decided to retreat and to search for him elsewhere.

Fury of Abu Jahl's Gang

The fury of the Quraish mounted high when they failed to trace the fleeing Prophet. An attractive reward of one hundred she-camels was immediately announced for anyone bringing him back alive.

Asma narrates that after the departure of the Prophet with her father, Abu Jahl came to their house along with a number of the Quraish rogues. They questioned her about her father's whereabouts. She said that she did not know. On this the vulgar Abu Jahl slapped her in the face so violently that her ear-rings flew off. The miscreants then fled away.

The angry Quraish organized a big hunt. Several chasing gangs went into operation. After three days of unsuccessful search the chasers' enthusiasm appeared to be waning. Meantime Abu Bakr brought the two camels which had been kept somewhere under the custody of a paid keeper. He offered the better of the two to the Prophet and requested him to ride it. The Prophet, however, refused to ride the camel that he did not own. When Abu Bakr offered the same as a gift the Prophet still insisted on paying the price. He bought the camel on payment. They then rode off on the fourth day. Abu Bakr carried Amir b. Fuhayra behind him as an attendant. Arqat had been specially engaged to act as guide for the historic journey which started on September 16, 621.

Jinn Signals the News

For sometime there was no news of the where-

101

abouts of Prophet's party. Then from the lower parts of Makkah was heard the voice of a Jinn (spirit). He was singing some verses in the characteristic Arab style. People listened to his voice and some even followed it. But they could not see the singer. The Jinn then emerged clear from the upper part of Makkah singing these verses:

"God the Lord of men give the best of His rewards
To the two companions who rested in the two tents.
They came with good intent and went off at nightfall.
May Muhammad's companion prosper!"

On hearing Jinn's verses Abu Bakr's family felt relieved to know that the two friends were heading safely for Madina.

Reward—Greedy Chasers

Suraqa b. Malik narrates an interesting episode. The Quraish's special reward of one hundred camels for anyone arresting Prophet Muhammad had intrigued many an adventurous man to try luck. One day while Suraqa was sitting in the company of his people one of his men came up and reported excitedly: "By God, I have just seen three riders passing. I think they must be Muhammad and his companions". Suraqa gave him a wink, enjoining silence. He then said dodgingly, "they are so and so, looking for a lost camel". "Perhaps so", said the other man and he kept quiet thereafter.

To avoid suspicion Suraqa remained there for a while. Then getting up he went straight to his house. He ordered his horse to be got ready. Then he asked

102

The pagan horse-riders in wild chase of the Holy Prophet.

for his weapons lying in the back of the room. He wore his armour and taking his divining arrows came out of the house. As he cast the divining arrows out came the arrow which he did not want. It read: "Do him no harm." He repeated the exercise but got the same result. Suraqa was utterly dismayed for he had hoped to capture the Prophet and to bring him back to the Quraish to win the covetted hundred camels reward.

Bad Luck for Suraqa

Ignoring the divining arrows he, however, decided to ride off in pursuit of luck. When his horse was gallopping fast it stumbled and he fell on the ground. Considering it somewhat unusual he resorted to the divining arrows again. Out came the same unpalatable result: "Do him no harm." The stubborn Suraqa had gone crazy after the all-too luring reward. He still continued the wild chase. His horse stumbled again and threw him on the ground once more. He tried the divining arrows again. The result showed no change. However, despite all those unfavourable indications he kept the chase with full zeal and zest.

Eventually he was able to see the Prophet's party from a distance. The game appeared to be nearing a fruitful end when his horse stumbled again. This time its fore-legs got stuck up into the dusty ground. Suraqa had fallen flat again. As his horse struggled hard to disengage its legs a thick screen of dust and smoke rose up like a sand storm.

The Deed of Security

Suraqa was now in a terrible mess. Reflecting over the queer chain of meaningful events he was eventually convinced that being protected against him by some unseen power the Prophet's party enjoyed the upper hand. He shouted, revealing his identity and asked them to wait for him. He assured them that he had no intentions to harm them.

The Prophet enquired from Abu Bakr to ask him what he wanted. Suraqa said, "write me a deed of security which will be signed between you and me." The Prophet instructed Abu Bakr to do the needful. Then Abu Bakr's servant, Amer, wrote the requisite document on a bone, or, as some other historians say, on a piece of paper, or a potsherd. It was thrown over to Suraqa. He put it in his quiver and galloped back discontinuing the chase.

Suraqa narrates that he kept quite about the entire episode until later on when the Prophet had conquered Makkah. Suraqa then appeared before him, showed him the document and embraced Islam.

Other Episodes on Way

Another chaser during this flight journey was Bareedah Aslami. He and his gang of seventy chasers had also been motivated by the big camel reward. But when they finally came face to face with the Holy Prophet their mental outlook took an entirely different turn all of a sudden. They embraced Islam.

Zubayr, who was returning from Syria along with a trade caravan also greeted the Prophet on the way. He presented him and Abu Bakr gifts of white dresses.

To dodge the chasers and to avoid suspicion or detection a much longer and tedious route along the coastline had been preferred to the usual, common and shorter one. Trekking through all those hazardous paths the Prophet's party eventually neared Madina, quite safe and sound.

Jubilant Welcome at Madina

The news had already reached Muslims of Madina that their loving Prophet had already left Makkah and was due to arrive any time. Eagerly expecting his arrival enthusiastic groups of Muslims used to go out of the town after morning prayers each day. They would keep waiting till the hot summer sun rose too high. The happy day dawned at last. The first man to spot him was a Jew. He called at top of his voice: "O Banu Qayla, your luck has come." Everyone then rushed to greet the Prophet who sat under the shade of a tree with his companion, Abu Bakr, sitting next. Most of the people crowding round him did not know which one of the two was the Prophet. As the shade under the tree vanished Abu Bakr rose in reverence to shield the Prophet from the scorching sun with the help of his mantle. This made it clear who was who.

The most memorable welcome to the Prophet was from a group of young children. They had been anxiously waiting for the arrival of a man they knew was the greatest lover of all children. They greeted him warmly with friendly gestures and sweet songs:

"Moon of the fourteenth night has risen on us at last
From behind the mountains on the south.
We must be grateful to the Lord
For the blessings of His religion and guidance."

The sweet melodies of the sweet welcome song echoed and re-echoed in the atmosphere. The Holy Prophet was simply delighted to see the children so

106

Young children welcoming the Prophet at Madina.

happy and so enthusiastic. He shook hands with them. He kissed them. He hugged them. He assured them that he had come to stay with them, to play with them and to guide them to a happier life.

QUESTIONS

1. What were the three deadly proposals against the Prophet which were discussed in the Town Hall meeting?
2. Why did the devil favour the proposal for instant assassination?
3. How did the Prophet manage to dodge the enemy and to escape from his house?
4. What arrangements had Abu Bakr made before their departure for the Thaur Cave?
5. How nature helped them while hiding at the Thaur Cave?
6. How did the Prophet console Abu Bakr when he felt afraid of the enemy approaching the cave?
7. How did Abu Jahl punish Abu Bakr's daughter when she did not furnish him the needed information?
8. How did the Jinn signal about the safety of the Prophet's party?
9. Describe Suraqa's bitter experiences during the futile chase.
10. What change for the better took place among chaser Bareedah and his gang?
11. How did the jubilant children welcome the Prophet outside the Madina City?

12

THE BATTLE OF BADR

To escape their pitiless persecution at the hands of Makkan pagans the great Prophet and his followers were obliged to migrate to Madina. They felt relatively far happier there and got enthusiastically engaged in the spread of Islam. In fact they were leading a far more effective and eventful life at Madina. The pagans of Makkah could not bear the sight of Muslims enjoying a peaceful and purposeful existence. They continued indulging in all sorts of intrigues and exercises to put a permanent end to the Prophet and his noble mission. A time came when they started active preparations for an invasion of Madina. They had established clandestine links with the pagans and Jews at Madina. Sometimes bands of Makkan pagans patrolled the outskirts of Madina. They harassed and robbed the local residents. They often lifted the cattle of the Muslims grazing in the pastures of Madina.

In a military expedition financial expenditure poses serious problems. In their war planning the Makkan aristocracy paid serious thought to this factor. They organized a huge trade caravan and deputed it to Syria under the leadership of their master brain, Abu Sufyan. Nearly everyone in Makkah contributed his share of goods to the big trade caravan. The idea was to earn maximum possible profits and to invest them on military action against the Madinite Muslims.

Rival Forces and Strategies

The Muslims had managed to get information about the wicked intrigues and war preparations of the enemy. The Prophet consulted his companions frequently over the problems of Madina's defence. One day the news broke into Madina that pagan fighting forces had already left Makkah and were on their way to invade Madina. The Muslims then mustered round the Prophet to adopt the requisite measures to meet the enemy threat. According to a hurriedly— chalked out two-pronged action plan it was decided:

(1) to capture the Makkan trade caravan which, by that time, was returning from Syria and was expected to pass through Madina any moment, and

(2) to engage the invading Makkans in a battle at Badr, a village on the outskirts of Madina.

The Prophet raised a small fighting unit of the Muslims and set out for Badr on Ramadan 12, 2 A.H. The Muslim unit totalled 313. The fervour of Jehad was at its peak. Even young children persisted to get enlisted. Meantime the enemy forces kept on advancing with great pomp and show. One of their apparent motives was to save their trade caravan returning home from Syria. Their strength exceeded one thousand which included one hundred mounted soldiers. Utbah, who at that time was the most honoured leader

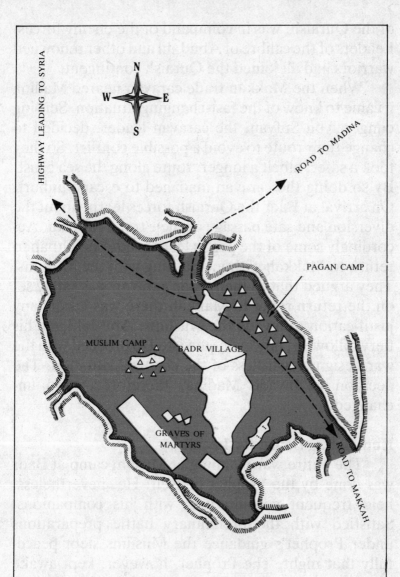

THE BATTLE OF BADR

of the Quraish, was in command of the enemy forces. Leaders of the calibre of Abu Jahl and other renowned warriors had all joined the Quraish contingent.

When the Makkan trade caravan neared Madina it came to know of the fast-changing situation. Sensing danger Abu Sufyan, the caravan leader, decided to change their route to avoid a possible conflict. So they took a safer, albeit a longer, route along the sea coast. By so doing the caravan managed to escape unhurt. On arrival at Badr the Quraish forces learnt about the diversion and safe passage of their trade caravan. Accordingly some of the pagan leaders advised Utbah to return to Makkah without clashing with the Muslims. They argued that as their trade caravan was safely set on the return route to Makkah there was hardly any justification to invade the Muslims. Abu Jahl and his fiery followers, however, persisted to proceed with the war designs regardless of the changed situation. The decision to invade Madina, therefore, stood unchanged.

Humiliating Defeat for Invaders

The entire war planning at Muslim camp at Badr was done by the Prophet himself. He, nevertheless, held frequent consultations with his companions. Satisfied with the preliminary battle preparations under Prophet's guidance the Muslims slept peacefully that night. The Prophet, however, kept awake throughout the night. He busied himself in prayers and meditation all the time. At dawn he assembled the forces for prayers. This was followed by his impressive sermon on Jehad. Thereafter the Prophet made a plan for defence positions by drawing lines on the ground with the help of an arrow. In all battle preparations considerable hue and cry is a routine phenomenon. The Prophet, however, directed that everything was to be done quite calmly and without unnecessary bal-lyhoo.

Then the zero hour arrived at last. Both the forces stood face to face with each other. The small unit of the Muslims had prayers on their lips. Their hearts overflowed with the light of faith. They stood behind their Prophet like one solid rock. On the contrary, the enemy forces entered the battlefield in characteristically flamboyant style. All along the way they had been indulging excessively in fun and frolic, music and mirth, women and wine and the like. The imbalanced ratio between the two forces stood at over three pa-gans to one Muslim. The ratio of war equipment was far more uneven.

The history-making battle started at last. According to the prevalent Arab custom noted individual warriors on either side were to challenge each other and to fight duels before the beginning of the general confrontation. It so happened that even during the preliminary duels Utbah, the pagan commander, fell to the sword of a Muslim challenger. Soon some of their other notables also lost their lives. Spectacular success in the initial bouts boosted the Muslim morale. When the regular fight started the enemy sustained further losses. Their pride for superiority in number of men, equipment and finances got shattered soon. Then Abu Jahl and many more of their notorious warriors fell in the field one after the other. This demoralized the enemy rather completely. They started to flee from the battlefield.

The handful of ill-equipped Muslim forces eventually emerged victorious. They had lost only fourteen men. None of the Muslims was taken prisoner. The enemy, on the other hand, lost as many as seventy men. Seventy of them were taken prisoner.

Griefs Marring Joys

A day before the return of the victorious Muslim forces to Madina Hadrat Zaid and Hadrat Abdullah dashed to the city to convey the news of victory of their people. They entered the city through different directions. Zaid rode Prophet's camel. His face was glowing with graceful glamour. As he waded through the welcoming crowds he went on narrating eye-witness account of the great Muslim victory and the humiliating defeat of the badly-routed enemy. The Muslims of Madina greatly enjoyed those fascinating details. The pagans, the Jews and the hypocrites, however, got terribly annoyed and upset. On hearing the accounts of the humiliation and slaughter of the pagans at Badr one of the Jewish chiefs yelled out in anguish: "After the slaughter of Arabia's real rulers and Kaabah's defenders death seems better than life."

The over-jealous Jews then hastened to hatch a cunning conspiracy to convert the jubilations of the victorious Muslims into anguish and agony. They generated a rumour that the Prophet had, as a matter of fact, been killed and the Muslims had actually been badly defeated at Badr. To lend support to their baseless rumour they manipulated a number of apparently –plausible clues. One such "indicator" was that Zaid had returned from the battlefield riding Prophet's camel. Had the Muslims been really victorious they

114

would have marched into the city victoriously with their Prophet riding his camel in front. The clever rumour-mongers further strengthened their canard by the more confounding argument that with the sudden "demise" of their loving Prophet and the crushing "defeat" of the Muslims Zaid had lost his mental balance. His imaginary accounts of the Muslim "victories" were an outcome of his sudden emotional shock.

Such vicious rumour-mongering proved considerably damaging. The joys of the Muslims of Madina began to turn into depression and agony. Luckily, however, the news of the Muslim victory soon started pouring in the town from all quarters. The rumours of Prophet's death and Muslim defeat were finally falsified. The grief-stricked Muslims became joyous and jubilant again. While they bowed their heads in thanks-giving prayers the necks of the rumour-mongering lobby were hung in shame and disgrace.

Unfortunately, however, a real grief of a great magnitude had also contaminated the victory jubilations. While the Prophet was leaving the city for the battlefield, his daughter, Ruqayyah, had fallen ill rather critically. She expired even before the return home of her victorious father. The Prophet and the entire Muslim community was tearful on that sad and untimely event.

Humane Treatment of Prisoners

Immediately after their defeat the badly-humiliated enemy started to flee away from the battlefield. The victorious Muslims, however, stayed in for sometime. They spent their time in collecting all the enemy corpses at one place. A big pit was dug and all dead bodies were buried in that collective grave. The Prophet had prohibited strictly the customary desecration of enemy's dead bodies. Inviting attention of his followers to the barbaric attitude in vogue with nations and governments of the world towards enemy casualties and prisoners he had condemned all such pre-Islamic brutalities.

The humane treatment meted out by the Muslims to Badr prisoners of war is simply unparalleled. The prisoners were divided into small batches and put under custody of the Muslims. They were instructed to take proper care of them and to treat them with affection and honour. Cases are on record where the custodians even abstained from eating in order to permit the prisoners to eat to their fill.

One of the notorious prisoners was Suhail b. Umr. He was a fiery orator. Before the Badr Battle he used to deliver combustible speeches against the Prophet in public meetings at Makkah. Pointing towards him Hadrat Umar once suggested the Prophet thus: "O Apostle of God, pull out two of his lower teeth so that he is unable to talk well." The Prophet declined to accept the proposal saying: "If I mutilate his organ God will do the same to me despite the fact that I happen to be a Prophet."

At a later stage the prisoners ransom money was settled at four thousand dirhams per head. The rich persons were asked to pay even more. But even those who could not pay the amount on account of poverty were set free. The literate prisoners were freed on making ten Muslims literate.

Considerable booty had also fallen to the lot of the Muslims during the Battle of Badr. The Prophet

116

got everything collected at one place. One-fifth of the entire lot was reserved for welfare works of the newly emerging state of Madina. The rest was distributed among the deserving Muslims. The share of the Badr martyrs was delivered to the bereaved families.

Flames of Wrath and Revenge

When the unexpected news of the Quraish's humiliating defeat reached Makkah the entire town plunged into deep grief and acute depression. Everyone felt bitter and revengeful. In order to boost the collective morale the indignant Quraish leadership put an indefinite moratorium on all mourning and lamentation for their dead in the battle.

A pagan chief, Aswad, had lost three of his sons in the battle, namely, Aqil, al-Harith and Zama Abu Hakima. He was so overwhelmed with grief and sorrow that his eyesight was gone. In the heart of his hearts he yearned to weep over his slain sons. But he had to keep a strict restraint on the flow of tears in compliance with the requirements of collective discipline. One night he heard someone crying in the streets. He thought the ban on mourning had perhaps been lifted. Being blind he asked his slave to go out and see who cried in the streets. "Is it a lamentation for the dead ones of the Quraish? Flames are afire in my heart too. If I too weep out a bit I shall feel better."

Soon the slave returned to report that it was a poor woman who was crying bitterly over a young camel she had lost. On this Aswad recited these verses:

Weep Not Over a Lost Camel!

"Does she weep because she has lost a camel?
And does this keep her awake all night?
Weep not over a young camel
But over Badr where hopes were dashed to the ground.
Over Badr the finest of the sons of Husays
And Makhzum and the clan of Abu'l-Walid.
Weep if you must weep over Aqil,
Weep for Harith the lion of lions,
Weep unweariedly for them all,
For Abu Hakima had no peer."

Suppressing free expression of their grief the Makkans went on burning within with the flames of wrath and revenge. That boosted their preparations for a return fight to avenge the loss and humiliation of the crushing blow at Badr.

Foundations of Culture and Civilization

Muslim victory in the Battle of Badr is a historically-significant event. After that victory Muslim predominance over the adjoining area became an established fact. The Makkan pagans had lost their political elite. Their military might had received a crushing blow. Their socioeconomic fabric had been shattered. In fact, they were utterly demoralized, disillusioned and dismayed. As against this the morale of the Muslims had shot up. Their authority was acknowledged and felt in all sectors of life in and around Madina. Solid foundations for effective functioning of a unique welfare state had been firmly laid by now.

The new state that began to emerge and evolve at Madina was destined to serve as the centre of civilization and culture of Islam. In the coming years the mallowing impact of that fascinating culture transformed the life and economy of the surrounding lands. In fact, a metamorphic change soon started to mould the minds of entire mankind. Then a time came when the whole of east and west got beautified by the flow of that revolutionary culture and civilization the seeds of which had been so firmly sown in the state of Madina.

QUESTIONS

1. Why were the Makkan pagans perturbed over the Muslims living peacefully at Madina?
2. What was the Muslim strategy for the Battle of Badr?
3. What differentiated the two rival forces when they entered the battlefield?
4. What were the war losses on both sides?
5. What griefs marred the joys of Muslim victory?
6. How did the victorious Muslims treat the prisoners of war?
7. How did the defeated Makkans keep the flames of wrath and revenge burning all the time?
8. How did the Badr victory lay the foundations of civilization and culture?

13

DEFEAT IN A WINNING BATTLE

After meeting their disastrous doom at Badr the pagans of Makkah were caught up in the flames of revenge and retaliation. They had lost the choicest of their leaders and statesmen. Their minds were haunted by the memories of the departed souls. Abu Sufyan had vowed that he would neither take a bath nor put oil on his hair till he had avenged their dead at Badr. Nearly every Quraish woman raised laments in memorium of her slain father, brother, husband, son or kinsfolk. The emotional atmosphere of Makkah was thus seriously charged with clouds of despair, despondency and desperation.

Emotional and Economic Crisis

To keep the fire of retaliation burning with full force their poets composed fiery verses of wrath and revenge and thus kept the emotions afire all the time. Said Umayya b. Abu'l-Salt:

Weep Over the Nobles!

"Would'st thou not weep over the nobles,
Sons of nobles, praised by all,
As the doves mourn upon the leafy boughs,
Upon the bending branches,
Weeping in soft dejected notes
When they return at nightfall.
He who weeps them weeps in real sorrow,
He who praises them tells the truth."

Along with this emotional upheaval a dreadful economic crisis hovered over Makkah. They had paid the Muslims over 2,50,000 dirhams as ransom money for release of their prisoners. The Syrian trade route had been lost after Muslim dominance over Madina. This had given a death blow to their foreign trade and commerce. The precarious state of Makkan economy had hit practically every household. Thus apart from the bitter emotional factor the unpalatable economic reality was also fuelling fast the flames of hatred and vengeance. The war preparations, accordingly, kept a high pace and exceptional zeal.

Makkans Invade Madina

Eventually when all preparations were finalized the Makkans were all set to invade the Muslims at Madina. A huge army, composed of 5,000 fighters was raised. It included 700 warriors wearing coats of mail, 200 horsemen and 3,000 camel riders. There was a special wing of women headed by Abu Sufyan's wife, Hind. The woman squad was inciting the warriors by singing fiery war songs. Hind recited the following verses to the beat of tambourines:

121

Hind's War Verses

"If you advance we hug you,
Spread soft rugs beneath you;
If you retreat we leave you,
Leave and no more love you."

The pagan forces marched from Makkah somewhere in 3 A.H. (625 A.D.) with traditional pomp and
show. On the way they passed by the grave of Prophet's mother at Abwa. Some infuriated troopers intended to demolish and desecrate it. The more sober
of the Quraish leaders, however, dissuaded them from
indulging in such outrageous acts. From Abwa the
troops reached Aqiq which is situated by the side of
Uhud Mountain, about 5 miles from Madina.

Counter Action by Muslims

The Muslims of Madina were receiving news of
enemy movements all the time. They were busy preparing for their defence. There were two schools of
thought over the mode of defence. One preferred to
fight the enemy while remaining within Madina. The
other was keen to face them outside the city. As the
majority favoured fighting outside the city, the Prophet preferred the latter mode. The decision taken,
the Muslims began to give final touches to their defence plans and preparations.

After the afternoon prayers that day the Prophet
wore his coat of mails. He hung his sword by the side.
With about 1,000 men behind him he eventually set
out for the battlefield. The defence enthusiasm was so
high that even children insisted to be enlisted. On the
way, however, the notorious hypocrite, Abdullah b.
Ubayy, retreated home along with his 300 men on a

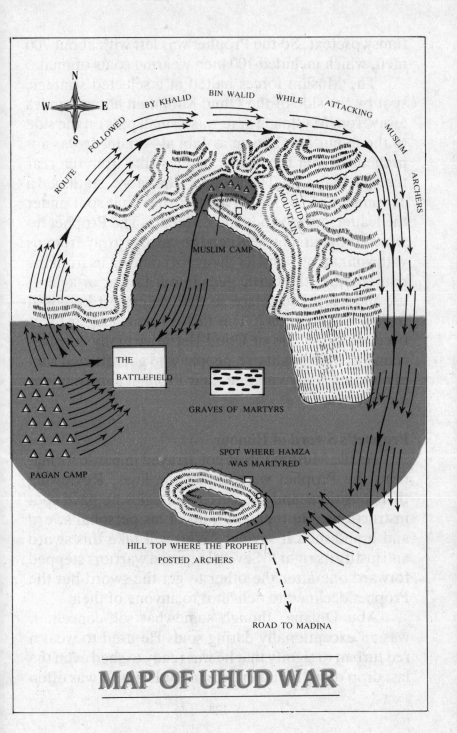

MAP OF UHUD WAR

flimsy pretext. So the Prophet was left with about 700 men, which included 100 men wearing coats of mail.

The Muslim forces halted at a selected strategic spot by the side of the Uhud Mountain about 3 miles away from Madina. There was a small pass on the side of the mountain, known as Jabl al-Ainain. It was apprehended that the enemy might strike from the rear through that pass. The Prophet, therefore, stationed a contingent of 50 trained archers over that spot under the leadership of Abdullah b. Jubair. The Prophet instructed the archers: "Keep the cavalry away from us with your arrows and let them not come on us from the rear whether the battle goes in our favour or against us; and keep your place so that we cannot be got at from your direction." This factor merits a clear focus because the whole of Uhud Battle virtually revolves round the sad plight of a people who got afflicted simply because they violated their Prophet's instructions on that issue.

Prophet's Sword of Honour

As the Muslim forces got arrayed in battle formations the Prophet went round the lines. Reviewing their positions and projected strategies he gave spot instructions. He then got hold of his personal sword and brandished it saying: "Who will take this sword and justify its right?" Several reputed warriors stepped forward one after the other to get the sword but the Prophet declined to deliver it to anyone of them.

Abu Dujana, though somewhat self-conceited, was an exceptionally-daring soul. He used to wear a red turban to signify that he was ready to shed even the last drop of his blood in defence of Islam. It was often referred to as "the turban of death." He got up and queried: "O Apostle of God, what is the right of the sword?" The Prophet answered: "That one should smite the enemy with it until it bends." Abu Dujana assured that he was willing to take the sword along with the obligation to fulfil its right. The Prophet was pleased to hand it over to him.

Having won a unique honour Abu Dujana brandished the sword up in the air with a sense of pride and prestige. Then he began to sing with joy:

The God's Sword

"I'm the man who took the sword
When 'use it right' was the Prophet's word.
For the sake of God, of all the Lord
Who doth to all their food afford".

Then referring to the enemy forces he vowed:
"Behind the ranks I'll never bide,
With God's own sword their ranks divide."

As he started to strut and swagger between the lines the Prophet remarked: "This is a gait which Allah hates except on an occasion like this."

Some Battle Scenes

After a short while both the forces took positions facing each other. The pagan forces far outnumbered the Muslims. They had far better equipment. They were motivated solely by the flames of hatred and revenge. On the other hand, the Muslim forces were inspired by a strong faith in sublime values and ideals. After the customary duels the general conflict started. Hadrat Hamza, Hadrat Ali and other Muslim warriors fought with exceptional courage and determination.

The enemy had been shaken to the core.

Brandishing the Prophet's sword of honour Abu Dujana also displayed unique feats of bravery. That deadly sword was flashing over the enemy like lightening. As he was so engaged his eyes fell on a pagan warrior who was attacking the Muslim ranks rather fiercely. Abu Dujana dashed towards him. Lifting his sword he was about to slash his head when the warrior started shrieking like a woman. Abu Dujana stared at him in amazement. He discovered soon that the crying warrior was in fact Abu Sufyan's wife, Hind in a male disguise. Sparing her life Abu Dujana turned his face aside saying that it would be disgracing the Prophet's sword of honour to drench it in a woman's blood.

Victory Changes into Defeat

Although the Muslim contingent was far smaller than the pagan forces its valiant warriors put in such a heroic resistance that the enemy was beaten badly. The power and precision of Muslim swordsmanship had shattered the invaders. Their stalwarts were falling one after the other. At last they lost all courage and hope. The band of women inciting them to fight was also besieged on all sides. The pagans had brought an idol to the battlefield for blessings. As fear and frenzy gripped their ranks that idol too had fallen on the ground in the ensuing panic. When they started fleeing away from the field in terror and turmoil they trampled the fallen idol under their feet.

In the Battle of Uhud the Muslims emerged victorious. A bigger and a better-equipped army of the Quraish got badly beaten by a handful of well-disciplined and inspired Muslims.

The invaders were soon on the run. The Muslims chased the fleeing enemy up to a certain point. Then giving up the chase abruptly they got busy in collecting the booty. The greed of war spoils dissuaded them to chase the stampeding enemy up to a reasonably-safe distance. When the unit of archers posted to guard the Uhud pass saw their fellow brethren amassing booty they too were overpowered by greed. They forgot all about Prophet's standing instructions about the defence of that sensitive strategic spot. They felt strongly inclined to slip away from the pass and to join the booty-grabbers. Their commandant warned them not to quit the post but it was all useless. Only a handful of the archers stood fast to the post. All the rest rushed to join the scramble for booty.

When the fleeing enemy found the Muslims all lost in collecting booty many of them started to halt and return to the battlefield. Meantime a fresh pagan unit led by Khalid b. Waleed (who had not yet accepted Islam) neared the Uhud pass. Finding the post poorly-manned he launched an offensive from that direction. When Khalid raised a loud war cry the morale of the straying enemy forces got a sudden boost. They all dashed to the battlefield. The few Muslim archers still guarding the pass failed to contain the on-rushing enemy forces. Putting in a heroic resistance they all fell one by one.

The battle scene started to change all of a sudden. A majority of the Muslims, however, was still lost in amassing the booty. They had hardly realized the fast changing texture of the situation. Like a sudden lightening the enemy forces overtook the disarrayed Muslims. Consequently, the very Muslim warriors who only a few moments back were chasing the fleeing pagans got entrapped on all sides by the encircling enemy.

Violation of Prophet's instructions about the defence of the strategic mountain pass had cost them too much.

Wahshi Kills Hamza

In the beginning of the battle the Muslims had enjoyed the upper hand by displaying great dare and discipline. Hadrat Hamza had fought very bravely. Even before that he had shown his worth in the Battle of Badr. The Quraish chiefs that he had killed at Badr included Utbah, the father of Hind. Since that day Hind was burning in the fire of revenge. Wahshi, a young Abyssinian slave of Jubair b. Mut'im, was skilled in the use of javelin. Hind had settled it with Wahshi that if he killed Hamza she would reward him richly. His master's uncle, Tuayma had also been killed at Badr. Jubair had also told Wahshi that if he killed Prophet's uncle, Hamza, in retaliation of his slain uncle, he would be set free.

Wahshi agreed to do the job. In fact, he had joined the Uhud Battle simply for that very purpose. When the battle began he started looking out carefully for Hamza. When he identified him from a distance Hamza was busy fighting like a valiant warrior. Hiding himself behind trees and rocks Wahshi started moving closer and closer towards him till he was sure that his target was within reach. He then poised his javelin and launched it at him. It pierced Hamza's body. Wounded critically Hamza began to stagger towards Wahshi in a vain attempt to hit him back. Wahshi then retired from the battlefield for that was all that he was supposed to do at Uhud.

Mutilation and Vengeful Verses

As the battle grew bloodier Muslims began to fall in greater number. Hind and her female companions went on a wild spree to desecrate and mutilate corpses of the Muslim martyrs. They chopped off their ears and noses and wove them into garlands. They wore them as anklets, collars and pendants and gave all their precious jewellery, that they were wearing that day, to Wahshi in lieu of his commissioned services. In a fit of rage Hind also split Hamza's belly and removed his liver. The vile woman then started to chew it. As she could not swallow the piece she spitted it out on the ground. Feeling a queer satisfaction from that beastly process she sat on a high rock and began to recite the following verses at the top of her voice:

We Have Paid You Back
"We have paid you back for Badr
And a war that follows a war in always violent.
I could not bear the loss of Utbah
Nor my brother and his uncle and my first-born.
I have slaked my vengeance and fulfilled my vow.
You, O Wahshi, have assuaged the burning in my breast.
I shall thank Wahshi as long as I live
Until my bones rot in the grave."

The vulgar woman also recited the following in her characteristic arrogant style:

When I Split His Belly
"I slaked my vengeance on Hamza at Uhud.
I split his belly to get at his liver.
This took from me what I had felt
Of burning sorrow and exceeding pain.
War will hit you exceeding hard
Coming upon you as lions advance."

Passing by Hamza's mutilated body the arrogant Abu Sufyan struck the side of his mouth with the point of his spear, yelling out contemptuously, "taste it, you rebel."

Rumour of Prophet's Assassination

The Muslim side was soon in a state of complete mess. Anguish and agony gripped their warriors. Hadrat Musaab b. Umair resembled the Prophet in outward appearance. He was killed by Qamia who then reported to Quraish that he had killed Muhammad. Soon the deadly rumour started to gain wider currency that the Holy Prophet had been killed. This demoralized the Muslim camp. Even men of the stature of Abu Bakr and Umar got disheartened. They threw their swords on the ground and sat stunned and sulking in a corner. The chaos and confusion that prevailed upset the mental balance of many a Muslim soldier. Some of them even killed each other mistakenly. Hadrat Huzaifa, for instance, lost his life at the hands of a Muslim.

The morale of the invading pagans had risen sky high. They were attacking Muslims from all sides. Their offensives were so severe that even the Prophet got wounded. His face was injured. He lost two of his front teeth. He bled profusely. Even then he kept his

130

balance and went on discharging his defence obligations. The pagans had dug a trap ditch in the battlefield. They had covered its mouth with straws and weeds. Evading the on-rushing enemy as the Prophet passed by that concealed ditch he slipped into it accidentally. Then Ali got hold of his hand and Talha helped him out.

While the rumour of Prophet's death was afloat some of his companions had surrounded him on all sides to shield him from the incessant enemy arrows and assaults. Then Hadrat Kaab happened to see him all of a sudden. He recognized him by his lovely teeth glittering beneath his helmet. He yelled out joyously: "O Muslims! Be happy. The Prophet is alive." The Prophet beckoned him not to make that declaration aloud. By that time, however, the Muslim warriors had all learnt about the falsity of the rumour about Prophet's assassination. They, therefore, rallied round him again and reorganized their ranks and files. Kaab's declaration had also been over heard by the pagan forces. Dismayed greatly they kept on attacking the Prophet from all directions. However, the Muslims had by now regained courage and confidence. A contingent of faithful guards protected the Prophet from all sides. Meantime, Ali, Ayesha, Fatimah and Abu Ubaidah Jarrah nursed his badly-bleeding wounds. At that moment Khalid's batch of dare-devil soldiers attacked him again. But the guarding Muslims obliged them to flee away.

The ordeal indeed was so taxing that the Prophet had grown too weak and too tired. He, therefore, offered the afternoon prayer at the Mount Uhud in a sitting posture. His companions too did the same.

Among the martyrs of Uhud was Ammarah b. Zaid. He bagged the unique honour of placing his cheeks by Prophet's feet while breathing his last.

Victory Intoxicating Invaders

Victory had intoxicated the arrogant invaders. At frequent intervals they raised slogans of joy and invoked the names of their honoured gods. They were happy that they had avenged their dead at Badr. As the battle subsided Abu Sufyan made this winding up declaration: "We have avenged ourselves fully of the humiliation at Badr. We will now settle accounts with you next year." The vile pagan women had continued their wild game of desecration and mutilation of the martyrs. Hind was going round proudly wearing garlands made of martyrs' mutilated organs. She had mutilated and disfigured Hamza's face beyond recognition. The Prophet felt deeply aggrieved over such wild deeds. But even then he ordered that no Muslim should indulge into such brutal acts even as a measure of normal retaliation.

The victorious pagans lost 20 warriors. They buried them and left the battlefield for Makkah. After that the Muslims got busy with burial of their casualties. The Uhud martyrs totalled 70.

Chasing the Retreating Enemy

Early next morning the Prophet reviewed the entire situation with his companions. It was decided to chase the pagan forces returning to Makkah. The idea was to boost the badly-shaken Muslim morale and to lessen the pangs of their anguish and agony through such daring measures. Accordingly, an advance unit of 70 men was despatched immediately. After some-time the Prophet also set out himself with the entire Muslim forces. They halted at a place, Hamra ul-Asad, about 8 miles away from Madina. At that time Abu Sufyan and his forces had halted at a nearby vil-lage, Rooha. The pagan forces seemed to suffer from a sense of frustration that they could not do the con-templated massive killing of the Muslims at the Battle of Uhud. They were accordingly considering post-ponement of their return to Makkah. They had almost decided to reattack Madina.

When they learnt that they were being hotly pur-sued by indignant Muslims they felt greatly perplexed. They could suffer a defeat in the second encounter. Fleeing away towards Makkah posed perils to pagan prestige and honour. While they were in that state of suspense Abu Sufyan hurled a psychological offensive at the chasing Muslims. He sent a threatening message that he was returning to give the Muslims a more crushing blow. The Muslim forces, however, were not the least deterred by the hollow threat. They fortified their position at Hamra ul-Asad and remained en-camped there for full three days, waiting for the threatened encounter. They lit huge fires at night time to make it clear to the pagan camp that they were too anxious for a return fight.

Abu Sufyan and his men were greatly dismayed and demoralized to witness the dare and determina-tion of the chasing Muslims. Calculating the pros and cons of the critical situation they thought it advisable to avoid a clash. They decided to continue their bro-ken journey to Makkah. Soon after that the Muslims too returned to Madina. The daring episode of the

Muslims chasing the returning victors somewhat boosted the Muslim morale. Their anguish and agony was lessened considerably. They set their minds to make up the losses sustained at Uhud. They began to prepare for future programmes with added hope and vigour.

Clouds of Grief and Enemy Taunts

The Muslims were terribly aggrieved over their defeat in a battle in which they had initially achieved a splendid victory. Madina city was in complete throws of grief and depression. As the loss of life was unexpectedly high the entire city was echoing with sobs and sighs of mourning. Grief-stricken ladies lamented the loss of their dear ones in louder wails. They often tore their attires, slapped their faces and raised tormenting hue and cry. This style of expressing grief over the dead was, in fact, a legacy of the pre-Islamic days. The Prophet discouraged all such unbecoming practices.

The Jews and hypocrites of Madina were jubilant over the pathetic plight of Muslims. They used to tease and taunt them rather frequently. The more vulgar of them even used to question them: "If the Muslim victory at Badr was a proof of Prophet's truthfulness, what did the Uhud debacle signify?"

The aggrieved Muslims bore all those insults and injuries with patience. They busied themselves in the stupendous task of post-war reconstruction and furtherance of their noble mission under their Prophet's versatile guidance.

QUESTIONS

1. Describe the crises which overtook the Makkans after their de-

feat at Badr?

2. What was the strength of the enemy forces which invaded Madina'?

3. What standing instructions were issued by the Prophet to the archers guarding the mountain pass during the Uhud Battle?

4. How did Abu Dajana win the Prophet's sword of honour'?

5. How was the Muslim victory at Uhud changed into a defeat?

6. Why did Wahshi kill Hamza?

7. What wild mutilation acts were committed by Hind'?

8. What happened when the rumour about Prophet's assassination gained currency?

9. Why did the Prophet decide to chase the victorious enemy returning to Makkah?

10. How did the Jews and hypocrites of Madina tease and taunt the defeated Muslims?

14

THE CONQUEST OF MAKKAH

After the Uhud debacle Muslims had devoted themselves to the stupendous task of restoring their lost power and prestige with a unique sense of dedication and determination. The profound policies pursued by the Holy Prophet (pbuh), his vigorous jehads and purposeful treaties contributed tremendously to rebuild the shattered fabric of the Muslims. The pace of constant reconstruction and reinvigoration eventually culminated in the re-emergence of the Muslims as a powerful community of upright people. The much-waited time arrived at last when the Prophet decided to lay a firm foot over atheism and idolatry so rampant in the holy city of Makkah. After crushing the roots of evil in an ancient cultural centre grounds were intended to be prepared to enable the entire Arabian peninsula to perceive and practise the Islamic way of life.

The Prophet was keen to fulfil this sacred obligation without the least clash or conflict. Although adequate preparation for the purpose had started the

Prophet took care that the information about his plans may not leak to Makkah so that the people there may not get panicky or hostile about it. At a later stage, however, he made a public declaration of his plans to visit Makkah. After that declaration the Muslims of Madina began to prepare for Makkah openly and with increased zeal and zest.

Prophet Arrives at Makkah

All necessary preparations were finalized soon. On Ramadan 10, 8 A.H. (February 1, 630 A.D.) the Prophet set out on the historic journey at the head of a large army consisting of 10,000 enthusiastic followers. It went on swelling on the way as representatives from various tribes kept on joining it in greater number. They arrived at Makkah on Ramadan 20, 8 A.H. (February 11, 630 A.D.). Being a seasoned statesman, a gifted general and an experienced traveller the Prophet had adopted such a winding and less-known route that the Makkans remained unaware of his moves for quite sometime. They came to know of his arrival when the Muslim forces had halted at Marr-uz-Zahran, a village situated just a mile away from Makkah. The tents of the Muslims got spread over a vast area in the surrounding territory. At night time when the warriors lit fires outside their tents the entire sandy tract gave appearance of a sparkling valley. The pagans were greatly impressed with the unusually enchanting spectacle.

Escorted by Hadrat Abbas when Abu Sufyan passed by Prophet's tent the guard post identified him quickly. Hadrat Umar had a mind to slash his head. But the Prophet pardoned him straightaway. During the brief conversation that ensued between the two, Abu Sufyan embraced Islam. He looked visibly repentant about the excesses and cruelties perpetrated by him on the Muslims during the span of his pre-Islamic career. Expressing his remorse and repentance he recited the following verses on that historic occasion:

"I Was Straying in the Darkness of Night"
"By the life when I carried a banner
To give   al-Lat's cavalry the victory over Muhammad
I was like one going astrary in the darkness of night,
But now I am led on the right track.
I could not guide myself, and he who with God overcame me
Was he whom I had driven away with all my might.
I used to do all I could to keep men from Muhammad
And I was called a relative of his, though I did not claim the relation.
I wanted to be on good terms with the Muslims.
But I could not join them while I was not guided".

Liberal Peace Drives
When Abu Sufyan was about to leave the tent the Prophet asked Hadrat Abbas to escort him to a lofty place on the mountains so that he could witness with his own eyes the grace and glory of the sprawling Muslims forces. Abu Sufyan was greatly impressed with the moving sight of a surging sea of determined men. Saad then remarked rather sarcastically: "There is

going to be a really conclusive battle today". Abu Sufyan's pride got hurt by these blunt remarks. Later when Prophet's special contingent happened to pass by he complained to him about Saad's taunting remarks. The Prophet paused for a while to console him saying: "Saad is totally wrong. Kaabah's lost prestige shall be restored today. This is the day for the restoration of peace for the aggrieved." The Prophet then continued marching further while reciting the *Surah Al-Fatha* (Victory).

Soon the Muslims forces encircled Makkah from all sides. Khalid b. Waleed (who had embraced Islam long time back) surrounded the city from the right side and Zubair b. Awam from the left. Abu Ubaidah was in command of the infantry.

On a meaningful appraisal of the prevailing situation the Makkans had at last realized full well that opposing the Muslims was now a futile exercise. Otherwise too being fed up of a perpetual tug of war they yearned for the restoration of law and order in a peaceful manner. They were weary of their sociocultural mess. As a sequel to the Muslim dominance over the Syrian high-way their trade and commerce had come to a virtual collapse. Nevertheless, even then there existed a thick-skinned group of evil-mongers and conspirators which was still bent upon clash and conflict. They had also organized a militant unit of seasoned vagabonds. Abu Jahl's notorious son, Akrama, was their leader. They had made Jabal Khandama as their mountanous headquarter. They even killed three noted warriors of Khalid's unit. On this Khalid got infuriated. He raided the gang and killed thirteen of them. The rest managed to flee away. In another case when a number of Quraish's conceited and conspiring leaders were beheaded, a huge heep of corpses got piled up. Seeing the pathetic scene Abu Sufyan yelled out in despair: "Quraish's green garden has been ruined."

Declaration of General Amnesty

The pagans of Makkah were apprehending severe reprisals for their past misdeeds. They felt extremely repentant of their criminal past. They were not quite certain of the type of treatment Muslims intended to give them. Clouds of uncertainty were soon dispelled when the Prophet addressed a big public gathering in the city. During that meeting he asked the people in a friendly tone: "What kind of treatment am I going to give you today?" They all replied in one voice: "You are a noble brother, son of a noble brother. Only good could be expected from you." On this the Prophet proclaimed: "Today you will not get any punishment from me. Feel quite free, all of you." This declaration of universal amnesty brought a glow of relief and happiness on people's tense faces. It was these very hardened people who had transgressed all normal limits in mounting murderous attacks on his life. They had left no stone unturned to abuse, humiliate, demoralize and torture him. Even the maximum punishment would have been no match for their past vulgarities and brutalities. The proclamation of a general amnesty brought an unexpected relief to their apprehensions and tensions.

The Prophet declared that the following categories of people shall get complete security and protection:

(1) those who enter the Holy Kaabah,
(2) those who surrender their arms,
(3) those who take refuge at Abu Sufyan's house, and
(4) those who close their doors and remain indoors.

Only 70 persons were exempted from the benefits of the general amnesty because they faced charges of extraordinary heinous offences. They were beheaded. That day Umme Hakeem, wife of Akrama b. Abu Jahl, also embraced Islam. Her delinquent husband, however, fled away to Yamen. Umme Hakeem followed him to Yamen and persuaded him to accept Islam. Bringing him back to Makkah she presented him before the Prophet. The Prophet pardoned him too.

Kaabah Cleaned of Idols

The basic object of the conquest of Makkah was two-fold: (i) to speed up dissemination of Islam, and (ii) to complete elimination of idolatry from the holy city of Makkah. By that time about 360 idols of varying sizes and descriptions had been installed within the precincts of Kaabah. The pagans used to worship them by going round them, supplicating them, offering them presents and the like. The walls of Kaabah were all filled with misleading and even insulting sketches of some prophets. Hubal was the most famous idol of Kaabah whom pagans considered as "the god of gods". Carved out of red ruby, its shape resembled that of a man. Seven sacred arrows remained lying near Hubal all the time. On these divining arrows the words "yes" (naam) or "no" (la) were inscribed.

After the conquest of Makkah the Prophet smashed all idols placed
in the Kaabah and piled the broken pieces outside the gate.

Whenever the superstitious Arabs intended to embark on a major project they drew lots through those divining arrows. They then acted strictly in accordance with the positive or negative direction indicated by the sacred arrows.

The Prophet smashed all those idols and statues into pieces. Holding a stick in his hand he gave fatal blows to all of them. While doing so he kept on reciting Quranic verses: "The truth has emerged and falsehood perished; certainly falsehood is indeed destined to perish" (Surah 17, Verse 81). Certain wooden pigeons had also been placed inside the Kaabah. He smashed them too. Some idols had been installed a bit high up. He felt difficulty in reaching them. He asked Ali to get on to his shoulders and to do the needful. Ali smashed all those humpty dumpty idols while taking his stand on Prophet's shoulders.

Kaabah also housed some misleading sketches and strange statues of some prophets and angels. The statues of Prophet Ibraheem and Prophet Ismaeel showed them holding gambling and divining arrows. The Prophet felt greatly hurt over such debasing exhibits. He remarked bitterly: "May God destroy the pagans, they knew that none of the two Prophets ever gambled." One of the Kaabah walls exhibited a large size of coloured painting of Prophet Isa. This too was erased. But the faint remnants of that painting remained visible for quite sometime even after Prophet's historic clean-up operation.

The pagans had also installed many huge statues in the suburbs of Makkah. Rituals resembling Hajj were performed around them. They too enjoyed the same sacrosanct status as the idols lying inside the

Kaabah. The most famed statues falling under this category were Lat, Manat and Uzza. The pagans believed that God resided with Lat in winter and with Uzza in summer.

The entire Arabian peninsula had been caught up in the tentacles of those idols, statues and paintings. It was Prophet's opposition to those all–too popular idols that the pagans had adopted an unfriendly and inimical attitude towards him. But their final day had arrived at last. They all met their doomed destiny with the conclusive blows of the greatest idol-breaker that humanity has ever known.

End of An Evil Era

Commemorating the day of conquest Fadala recited these verses regarding Prophet's clean-up operations:

God's Light Becomes Manifest
"Had you seen Muhammad and his troops
The day the idols were smashed when he entered
You would have seen God's Light become manifest
And darkness covering the face of idolatry."

All the phases of the conquest of Makkah were finalized quite expediently and gracefully. The victorious Muslims grabbed no booty. They did not allow others either to indulge in loot, arson or indecency. When the Holy Kaabah was relieved completely of the filth of debasing idols, statues, sketches and paintings the Prophet directed Hadrat Balal to chant the adhan. This was followed by the first ever congregational prayer inside the Kaabah after the historic clean-up. It was led by the Holy Prophet. To celebrate the great occasion the Muslims bowed their heads in thanks and gratitude to God Almighty.

The conquest of Makkah was the last instalment of that creative series of crusades which had initially started from Makkah itself. On that auspicious day even the most hardened rouge was granted a liberal pardon. The whole of the city got lit up which the light of Islam without clash or conflict. The Prophet stayed in Makkah for a total of about two weeks. During that short stay he gave final touches to all of his noble plans and projects.

The most memorable dimension of the fall of Makkah is the fact that the Holy Kaabah was relieved of the pernicious pollution of countless idols, statues, sketches and paintings which were a slur on its fair name and original role. By granting amnesty to the high and low the victorious Muslims founded an healthy tradition which could serve as path-blazing for all victors to come.

After the conquest of Makkah the Muslims continued their tableegh and jehad missions in and outside the Arabian peninsula with characteristic zeal and determination. Consequently the radiance of Islamic values and ideals went on spreading in all directions.

QUESTIONS

1. How did the Prophet set out on his historic journey to Makkah?
2. What did Abu Sufyan say after embracing Islam?
3. How did the Muslims handle the evil-mongers and the conspirators?
4. Who were granted complete security and protection according to general amnesty?
5. How did the Prophet clear Kaabah of age – old idols, statues and paintings?
6. What were the distinctive features of the Muslim conquest of Makkah?

15

A UNIQUE CHARTER OF LOVE AND PEACE

After the conquest of Makkah the light of Islam had begun to illuminate the entire Arabian peninsula with an amazing speed. Prophet's sovereignty was eventually acknowledged everywhere. Practically all Arab tribes had by now turned away from idolatry. They found it far satisfying to bow before One God. Only a few years back those very pugnacious creatures were at logger heads with each other. They were deeply entangled in all sorts of feuds and genocidal brutalities. The moment they came under the folds of Islam their hearts were cleansed of all pollutions of hatred and hostility. Those very swords which earlier used to be drawn so recklessly even over petty problems and personal vendettas now got devoted to dissemination of civilization and culture, defence and development of humanity.

The Historic Hajj Caravan

During the last decade of Zilqaadah, 10 A.H. the

146

Prophet was seen preparing for Hajj. Then he ordered others to prepare to accompany him. On this the mood of the entire area took a cheerful and festive turn. Enthusiastic people from mountains, vallies, plains and deserts began to flock Madina in greater numbers in a quest for Prophet's company in his intended Hajj journey. Soon a large city of tents began to emerge all around Madina. The number of intending pilgrims was around 90,000. These very people had earlier been caught up in the quagmires of enmity and violence. But now they looked like brothers eternally-united in immortal bonds of affection and love. Their heads and hearts had revolted against all evil and ignorance. They had all been united under the rule of One God.

Leading the sea of men surging with brotherly love the Prophet left Madina for Makkah on 25th Zil-qaadah, 10 A. H. (23rd February, 663 A.D.). When the great caravan arrived at Zul Khalifah the Prophet ordered a halt. They spent the night there. The entire caravan wore ehrams (the Hajj uniform comprising two simple cloth pieces). That great spectacle of human fraternity and equality was simply enchanting. When all members of that moving multitude wore the same simple uniform it presented an inspiring sight. The artificial barriers between high and low had all vanished in toto.

Performance of Hajj Rites

After donning the ehram the caravan proceeded further reciting takbeers on the way. The entire atmosphere resounded with sounds of Allah-o-Akbar. They reached Makkah on the 4th Zilhajj, after a con-

stant journey of nine days. With so many people join-
ing on the way the total by now had swelled to 140,000.
The Prophet went straight to the Kaabah. Kissing the
Black Stone he went round the holy place seven times.
He offered prayers at Muqam-e-Ibraheem and kissed
the Black Stone a second time. Then he went to the
Safa Mount and performed sayye (swift walking in
between Safa and Marwa).

On 8th Zilhajjah the Prophet left Makkah for
Mina. He pitched his tent at the Arafat grounds and
encamped there for the night. Next day he offered the
morning prayers. Then riding his she-camel, Qiswa,
he headed for Arafat Mount. By the time he had
climbed atop the mountain the audience around him
had increased further. The entire surrounding was re-
sounding with thunderous takbeers.

Manifesto of Love and Peace

As the sun was moving towards the west the
Prophet arrived at the Arafat grounds. While still sitting on his she-camel he gave the eager audience a historic address. It came to enjoy immortal fame in history as the greatest manifesto of love and peace. The
audience being unusually big a novel method of trans-
mission was adopted. When the Prophet completed a
sentence he observed a momentary pause during
which Rabia b. Umayyah repeated the same sentence
aloud and so on. That made it easy for the big audience
to listen and understand all that the Prophet was saying.

The main stream in Prophet's historic address ran
as follows. After praising and glorifying God he said:
"O men, listen to my words, I do not know whether

148

I shall ever meet you in this place again after this year. Your blood and your property are sacred as this day and this month are holy. You will surely meet your Lord and He will ask you about your doings. I have informed you. He who has a pledge let him return it to him who entrusted it to him. All usury is abolished. But you have a right over your capital. Wrong not and you shall not be wronged. God has decreed that there is to be no usury and the usury of Abbas b. Abdul Muttalib is abolished totally. All blood sheds of pagan period are to be left unavenged. The first claim on blood I abolish is that of Rabia b. al-Harith b. Abdul Muttalib (who was fostered among the Banu Layth and whom Hudhayl killed). It is the first blood shed in the pagan period which I deal with. Satan despairs of ever being worshipped in your land. So beware of him in the matters of your religion.......

You have rights over your wives and they have rights over you. You have the right that they should not disgrace you and that they should not behave with open indecency. If they do, God allows you to reform them and to punish them but not with severity. If they refrain from these evils they have the right to their food, clothing and affection. Treat them very kindly, for they depend upon you and enjoy lesser liberty. You have taken them only as a trust from God. You have the right to enjoy their company as directed by God. So understand my words, O men, for I have informed you. I have left with you something which if you hold fast to, you will never fall into error. It is: the Book of God and the practice of His Prophet. So give good heed to what I say.

Know that every Muslim is a Muslim's brother and that all Muslims are brothers. It is only lawful to take from a brother what he gives you willingly. So wrong not each other. O God, have I not conveyed?"

In the whole history of civilization and culture Prophet's farewell address is remembered as the greatest charter of love and peace for all times to come.

A Novel Communication Method

The entire audience listened to the address in rapt attention. The Prophet was keen that everyone should understand the letter and spirit of the great message and to make it a point to practise it in daily life. In order to make the communication more clear and more interesting he punctuated the address with periodic questions and answers, e.g.:

Prophet: Do you know what day is today?

Audience: It is the day of the Greatest Pilgrimage.

Prophet: Then remember that God has made your blood and belongings sacred for each other just as he had made this day and this month sacred for you all.

Towards the end of the great address the Prophet asked the audience: "Have I conveyed you God's message?" Loud voices went up in the air on all sides: "Certainly," "Certainly". On this the Prophet looked towards the sky with satisfaction, saying thrice: "O God, bear witness that I have fulfilled my obligation".

The Completion of Islam

The address over the Prophet stepped down his camel and offered the combined noon and the afternoon prayers. Then he rode the camel again and went to Sakhrat. The following Quranic verses were revealed to him there:

"Today have I completed your Faith for you,
And have completed My bounties for you,
And have approved Islam as the religion for you."
(Surah 5, Verse 3)

The Prophet hastened to communicate the revealed verses to the people. When Abu Bakr listened to the verses he broke into tears. He was a man of vision. He realized almost instinctively that when the religion had been finalized and the Prophet had fulfilled his sacred obligations then his departure from the immortal world must as well be imminent.

From the Arafat the Prophet moved to Muzdalfah. He stayed there for the night. After the morning prayer he left the place. On his way he performed rami (stone-throwing at the devil) and returned to his tent at Mina. While starting from Madina he had brought one hundred sacrificial camels with him. He sacrificed 63 of them, one for each year of his life. The remaining 37 were sacrificed by Hadrat Ali. Finally the Prophet got his hair cut. When all the Hajj rites had been performed the Prophet and all the followers took off the ehrams and wore the usual dresses.

Different Names of the Last Pilgrimage

This memorable Hajj has been immortalized in history by various names, e.g.:

(1) The Farewell Pilgrimage (Hajj tul—Wida),

(2) The Pilgrimage of Islam (Hajj tul–Islam),

(3) The Pilgrimage of Dissemination (Hajj tul–Tableegh),

(4) The Greatest Pilgrimage (Hajj tul–Akbar), etc.

As a matter of fact each one of these names has a relevance and a meaning of its own. The pilgrimage was a farewell congregation because it was the last Hajj of the Holy Prophet. After that he could not get another opportunity to visit Makkah and to perform tawaf of the Holy Kaabah. It was the Pilgrimage of Islam because the official declaration of completion of Islam was made during that Hajj. The Pilgrimage of Dissemination is also an appropriate name because it was during that Hajj that the Prophet conveyed all those essential instructions to people which God had ordered him to. The Greatest Pilgrimage is an equally befitting name for such a grand Hajj had never been performed before nor shall one like that be ever performed till eternity.

QUESTIONS

1. How did people become cheerful and festive when the Prophet declared his intention to proceed for Hajj?

2. Give a brief description of the Hajj rites?

3. Why is Prophet's Last Sermon remembered as the greatest charter of love and peace?

4. What novel communication method was adopted during the Last Sermon?

5. What famous Surah was revealed after the Last Sermon?

6. What are the different names given to Last Pilgrimage?

16

DEATH OF THE GREAT BELOVED

After laying solid foundations of human guidance, welfare and development Prophet's revolutionary mission had been fulfilled. It appears he had known by then that he was about to leave the mortal world. Somewhere during June, 632 A.D. he paid a midnight visit to Madina's famed cemetry, Janat-ul-Baqui, along with his freed slave and a close friend. After offering fateha at the graves the Prophet flashed a feeler that he was soon going to greet his Lord. Around 11. A.H. he started preparing for the final journey in a rather serious manner. His prayers and meditations went on prolonging day by day.

The great Prophet knew full well that people cherished immense love and devotion for him. In order, therefore, to prepare them for the forthcoming separation and the consequent bereavement shock he started using a variety of wise techniques. During the Farewell Pilgrimage he had made this bold reference: "I may not be seen here during the next Hajj." Earlier once while offering fateha for the martyrs at the Uhud

The Baqui Graveyard which the Holy Prophet visited at midnight
shortly before death.

Mountain he had thus addressed the departed souls: "I shall join you soon." Sometime after his return from the cemetry he had made a clear-cut announcement about his imminent departure. Hardly a few days before his death while addressing a big public gathering at Madina he had blessed the audience with some valuable advices. In that very meeting he had also alerted them about his forthcoming transition. That indeed was his last public address.

Agonies of Death Disease

The Prophet had since long been complaining of some physical pain. During June, 632 A.D., however, that persistent pain assumed an acute intensity. On Monday, 29th Safar, 11 A.H., when he returned home after attending a funeral, the pain had become rather unbearable. When one of his companions enquired about it the Prophet had remarked: "No other persons undergo more pain than the Prophets. That is why their recompense is also greatest." The duration of the last illness stretches to about 13 to 14 days. He kept on visiting the Prophet's Mosque for the first eleven days during which he led the prayers rather regularly. Five days before death once while fever and pain touched their peak the Prophet desired to have a cold bath. He ordered that seven skins full of water be obtained from different wells of Madina for that purpose. The cold bath lowered his temperature considerably and he felt sufficient relief. Then he went to the mosque and addressed the audience. He instructed them, *inter alia,* that after his death his grave was not to be turned into a seat of worship.

By the time he returned home the pain was growing acute again. He looked very weak and exhausted. Some Muslims returning from Abyssinia had brought a medicine. While the Prophet lay in coma Hadrat Abbas administered him a doze of that medicine. When the Prophet regained consciousness he expressed his displeasure over the administration of medicine without his prior approval. He then directed that all those present on the occasion be administered the same medicine as a sort of an interesting punishment.

"Abu Bakr Not Umar"

When his illness took a more serious turn he directed that Abu Bakr should lead the prayers in his place. Abu Bakr had the unique honour of leading 17 prayers while the Prophet was critically ill. Hadrat Ayesha narrates that when the Prophet instructed Abu Bakr to lead the prayers during his fatal illness she had raised some objections. She had said that her father was a man of delicate constitution and had a feeble voice. He was frequently overpowered by emotions while reciting the Holy Quran and his eyes got drowned in copious tears. Otherwise too Ayesha apprehended that people would not tolerate another man leading the prayers while the Prophet was still alive. On these grounds she did not consider it advisable that Abu Bakr be asked to lead the prayers. The Prophet, however, over-ruled her objections.

An interesting event happened during those days. Once while Balal had chanted the adhan the Prophet asked someone to get hold of the leader for the prayer. Abdullah b. Zaman went in search of Abu Bakr. He failed to find him anywhere. As chance would have it he came across Umar on the way. He requested him to lead the prayer. Umar agreed readily. But the moment he uttered Allah-o-Akbar the Prophet recognized his characteristically-loud pitch. He directed at once: "Abu Bakr, not Umar, shall lead the prayer." While Umar continued with the prayer hunt for Abu Bakr was restarted. He was eventually traced out. But by the time he arrived at the mosque Umar had already finished the prayer.

Umar got greatly aggrieved of this comedy of errors. Clarifying his position he remarked that when he was asked to lead the prayers he thought it was under Prophet's instructions. On this Abdullah offered his regrets saying: "When I could not find Abu Bakr anywhere I thought that in his absence you were the next best person to lead the prayer."

His Last Day on Earth

The Prophet freed all his slaves on Sunday, a day before his death. As a matter of fact those slaves were already leading a free life for they had been extended rights and privileges rarely enjoyed even by free persons. His coat of mail had ben pawned with a Jew for a certain quantity of barley. The remaining articles of his arms were donated to the Bait-tul-Maal.

The total amount that he had in cash was 7 dinars. He had instructed to distribute the entire amount in charity. During disruption in the routine household affairs following the fatal illness his direction about the dinars slipped Ayesha's mind. When he got a moment of relief he enquired about the money. Ayesha reported that the money was still lying with her. He ordered the dinars to be placed before him. Then he held the coins in his hands and said: "If these dinars were to remain unspent with what justification could I appear before my Lord?" The money was then distributed immediately among the needy.

On that historic night Ayesha did not have enough oil at home to light the lamp. She had, therefore, to borrow some from a neighbouring lady. The last night lamp at the great Prophet's house was thus lit with borrowed oil.

Last Words and Last Kisses

On that very day while lying on death bed he removed the door curtain aside to have a peep at the mosque in front. Abu Bakr was leading the prayer. He felt extremely delighted over the pleasant spectacle. He had already slept well during the previous night. Charming freshness had returned to his graceful face. As he felt a bit better he went to the mosque, supported by Abbas and Ali.

On return from the mosque his condition began to deteriorate again. Lying in Ayesha's lap he sent for his loving daughter, Fatimah Batool. When she arrived he whispered slowly into her ear: "I am about to leave the world." The second whisper that he made said: "Among the family members you would be the first lady to greet me in Paradise." Finding the father gripped by acute agony Fatimah started crying. The Prophet forbade her to do so. Then he sent for his grandsons, Hasan and Hussain. He kissed them. Meantime his condition kept on deteriorating further. In that tormenting state he was heard uttering such words of guidance as: "prayers, prayers and your slaves."

The 8th June was an extremely hot day. Close to

his death bed had been placed an earthen jar containing cold water. The Prophet put his hands into it every now and then and rubbed the moisture over his head. Meantime, Abu Bakr's son, Abd ar-Rahman, called in. He held a freshly-cut miswak. The Prophet gestured Ayesha that he wanted to have the miswak. Ayesha got hold of it, softened the top by chewing it under her teeth and then placed it in Prophet's hand. He kept on rubbing it over his teeth quite energetically for a while till it got slipped from his hand. At a much later date Ayesha recollected the incident by remarking: "Even on that memorable day too God united the mucus of the two of us."

Before he went into the final expiating coma the last words that were heard coming out of his lips were:

(1) "May God destroy those people who convert their prophets' graves into places of worship," and

(2) "Let not two religions (Judaism and Christianity) remain on the soil of the Arabian peninsula."

And then on Monday, 12th Rabi ul-Awwal, 11 A. H. that sad event at last took place which his devotees had been apprehending for quite sometime in the past. Ayesha thus narrates the last moments of that doleful event: "He began to gasp while still in my lap. I felt that his body became very heavy all of a sudden and his hands got loosened. When I looked at his face I found that his eyes were getting fixed......" The saddest moment of history had eventually arrived. On the afternoon of that sad Monday humanity lost its most memorable lover ever born anywhere on this planet:

"We all come from God

And to Him do we return!"

He was eight days less 63 years on that mournful Monday when he breathed his last. Indeed Monday has a unique significance in his life span. He was born on Monday. He had settled the great Black Stone dispute on Monday. He was elevated to prophethood on Monday. He migrated from Makkah on Monday. He arrived in Madina on Monday. And he left us too on Monday.

Confusion Before Burial

The news of Prophet's death spread like wild fire in the whole of the Arabian peninsula. The Muslims were engulfed in a nightmare of despair and despondency. Hadrat Umar simply refused to believe in the stunning news. Abu Bakr had gone to visit his wife outside Madina. When he heard the sad news he got on a fast-moving camel and rushed to Madina. He found Umar delivering a fiery speech to the effect that the Prophet had not died. Simultaneously, however, pathetic sobs and sighs were rising incessantly from Ayesha's apartment.

Getting down the camel Abu Bakr dashed straight into Ayesha's chamber. He was fully convinced of Prophet's death. He came out hurriedly and thus addressed the bewildered audience: "O men, if anyone worships Muhammad, then Muhammad is certainly dead. But if anyone worships God, God is alive, immortal." On this everyone, including Umar, began to realize that the Prophet had, as a matter of fact, died. Finding no way out but to practise patience the stir and commotion of the shocked audience eventually began to subside gradually.

Meantime information was received that Saad b. Abadah was mustering supporters in a community hall in a desperate bid to get himself declared as Prophet's successor. Abu Bakr and Umar rushed to the spot. Combustible speeches were being delivered over there. The situation seemed to be going beyond control. However, the two great statesmen handled the situation wisely. They brought the matter under control. With consensus of the majority it was soon decided that Abu Bakr be declared the First Caliph. All Muslims swore oath of allegiane to him in Prophet's Mosque. In his inaugural address on the very first day Abu Bakr announced: "If I follow God and His Apostle you too obey me. But if my words and deeds betray a disobedience to God and His Apostle then my obedience is not obligatory upon you."

Last Wash and Last Glimpses

After the declaration of Hadrat Abu Bakr's Caliphate and the oath of allegiance the situation returned to normalcy. The Muslims then turned to arrangements for Prophet's burial. Ali, Abbas, his two sons (Al-Fadal and Qusman), Usama and Prophet's freed slave, Shurqan, participated in the last wash. A bedouine, Aus b. Khauli, had been Prophet's companion in the Battle of Badr. He requested Ali for permission to participate in the last wash. The permission was granted.

That day was terribly hot and humid. Owing to the dissension prevailing in the Muslim ranks Prophet's dead body had remained without wash and burial for quite a long period of time. Despite that, however, the body kept on emitting fragrant smells all

161

the time. After the last wash the body was wrapped up in the coffin. It was then placed on a cot and kept in state for final glimpses and homages by the aggrieved Muslims. The general glimpse continued for quite a long time. Visitors entered Prophet's residence from the door towards the mosque side. They went out through the other door after paying last homages.

When Abu Bakr and Umar entered in the emotional atmosphere assumed a more moving magnitude. In an exceptionally respectful tone Abu Bakr paid homages to the body lying in state. He also gave a brief address to console the mourning visitors. This comforted the disheartened Muslims and lessened somewhat their load of grief and depression.

The place where the Prophet's body lay in state was a narrow one. Hence one big funeral prayer could not be organized. Mourners went in batches of ten to offer the funeral prayers. Then when they came out the next batch of ten entered in and so on.

Moving Burial Episodes

Many petty controversies had arisen immediately after Prophet's demise. In which city should his body be buried? Three alternatives came under consideration: (a) Bait al-Maqdas, (b) Makkah, and (c) Madina. After a lot of discussion decision was made in favour of Madina. The next question that loomed large centred round the precise place of burial in Madina. Again three proposals were mooted: (i) near the graves of his companions, (ii) near the pulpit of Prophet's Mosque, and (iii) inside Ayesha's Hujra. Eventually the last-mentioned place was selected. The issue of the shape of the grave also evoked debate.